TO ALL THE GREAT WOMEN IN MY LIFE—
YOU KNOW WHO YOU ARE.

ALL I CAN SAY IS THANK YOU.

TABLE OF CONTENTS

My food isn't fussy, and neither am I. That may be a little tough to believe, given that one of the places I'm best known as a chef is on *Hell's Kitchen*, the TV show on which you can pretty reliably expect Chef Gordon Ramsay to yell at everyone around him when things aren't perfect. And yet, from my perspective, perfect food is just, well . . . whatever *you* want your food to be.

If you like your lobster risotto richer than how I tell you to make it in this book, I say go for it. If you want to swap in crab for lobster or scallions for chives, then hey: Cool. I'm not the food police—I'm never gonna show up in your kitchen and tell you you're doing it wrong. The recipes in this book don't need to be followed exactly. I always say that cooking isn't rocket science; it's about making cold food hot. And above all, it's about really and truly enjoying the food we cook and eat.

And a big part of that enjoyment means embracing how we actually cook at home. My daily work life cooking in my restaurants and on TV is what I'd call "controlled chaos." There, I'm used to cooking under pressure, sometimes for lots of people at once. (For a handful of those TV recipes, see the Prime Time Recipes chapter on page 53.) But then, once I'm home and relaxed, I make the foods in this book because, frankly, they're an antidote to all that pressure.

So while my first book, *Buttermilk & Bourbon: New Orleans Recipes with a Modern Flair* (which, by the way, you should *definitely* run out and buy immediately) was driven by the menus of two of my restaurants, the book you're reading right now is geared toward home cooks like . . . well, like me. That means recipes that are simple, quick, and delicious—but that still have an element of pro-cheffy-ness to them in their creativity, presentation, and strategic make-ahead techniques.

These dishes also represent how my whole blended crew at home lives and eats. Half of my family is Irish and the other half is Portuguese. My wife and in-laws are 100% Vietnamese. So we make egg rolls (page 64) as an appetizer on Thanksgiving, eventually followed by my Nana's apple pie (page 108) for dessert. And on the regular, we lean toward dishes that are easily shared by everyone (see Mixed Family Style on page 61).

All in all, these are relaxed-but-refined recipes that hopefully take the pressure to be perfect off of home cooks, but keep the flavors and enjoyment on. Honestly, cooking like this in my home at the end of my day is a godsend for me and something I want to share with you. So by all means, dig in. . . .

BEFORE
– YOU –
ENTER

Whatever you do, don't let anyone tell you that appetizers aren't a crucial part of any meal. Just the opposite: A great opener kicks things off like a big ol' firework, setting off your appetite and an explosion of flavors, and maybe most importantly, catalyzing expectations for what's to come for the rest of the meal. I love it when I cook someone an appetizer that surprises them—makes them sit up and take notice, and just gets them revved from the get-go. The following dishes do just that with big, fresh flavors that hint at what's to come, but would also be worthy of excitement even if they were the only thing being served.

QUICK FRIED CALAMARI

with Orange-Garlic Gremolata and Basil Aioli

SERVES 6-8

ORANGE-GARLIC GREMOLATA

1 clove garlic, minced

2 tbsp (8 g) minced parsley

1 tbsp (5 g) freshly grated horseradish

2 tsp (4 g) orange zest

BASIL AIOLI

1 cup (240 ml) mayonnaise

2 tsp (10 ml) Dijon mustard

2 tsp (10 ml) red wine vinegar

1 clove garlic, minced

2 tbsp (6 g) minced basil

S&P Mix (page 133), to taste

CALAMARI

2 cups (250 g) all-purpose flour

1 tbsp (6 g) lemon pepper

1 tbsp (7 g) smoked paprika

¼ tsp cayenne pepper

1 tsp salt

1 tsp white pepper

Canola oil, for frying

1½ lb (680 g) calamari, rings and tentacles

1 cup (240 ml) buttermilk

S&P Mix (page 133), to taste

10–12 cherry tomatoes, quartered

1 lemon, cut into wedges, for garnish

I have this undying love for fried calamari. It's one of those things that, if I see it on a menu, I've just gotta have it. I especially love versions like this one, that are simple enough to let the fresh calamari flavor and texture shine, with just a few slight enhancements. The crazy thing about fried calamari in general is that, while it's very economical to make at home, it can get pretty expensive at a restaurant. With this recipe, you get the budget-friendliness of making it yourself, while also eating one of the best versions around.

Make the gremolata: Mix all ingredients together in a bowl and set aside.

Make the basil aioli: Mix all ingredients together in a bowl, season with S&P Mix, and set aside.

Make the calamari: Mix the flour, lemon pepper, paprika, cayenne, salt, and white pepper together and set aside. To cook the calamari, heat 2 inches (5 cm) of canola oil in a in a straight-sided pot. Check the temperature with a thermometer; it will be ready when it reaches about 350°F (177°C).

Toss the calamari in the buttermilk and then drain off the excess. Toss it in the seasoned flour mix until it's well coated. Shake off excess flour. Fry the calamari in batches for 1 to 2 minutes. Make sure not to overcook it—wait just until it's golden brown. When the calamari is cooked, drain it on paper towels and season with S&P Mix.

Place the calamari on a plate and sprinkle the gremolata over the top, along with the cherry tomato quarters. Garnish with the lemon wedges and serve immediately with the basil aioli for dipping.

HOT OR COLD PEEL-AND-EAT SHRIMP COCKTAIL

with Red Remoulade

SERVES 4 AS AN APPETIZER

8 cups (1.9 L) water

¼ cup (29 g) Old Bay® or Zatarain's® seasoning

¼ cup (27 g) Cajun Spice (page 137)

4 lemons, 2 cut in half and 2 quartered, divided

2 bay leaves

1 bunch parsley, chopped, about 10 sprigs reserved

1 (12-oz [355-ml]) bottle beer

1 onion, diced large

¼ cup (60 g) minced garlic

½ cup (120 ml) Crystal® hot sauce

1 cup (240 ml) Red Remoulade (page 145)

1 lb (454 g) shrimp, shells on and sized 21/25

½ cup (114 g) butter, melted (if serving the shrimp hot)

Peel-and-eat shrimp cocktail, if made properly, is both simple *and* fancy. It's super fun to eat and is about a hundred times more flavorful because the shell adds a depth of flavor to the shrimp meat. Isn't a ribeye better on the bone? Well, it's the same idea with shrimp. So get your martini shaker out, people: We're having the very best kind of shrimp cocktail at home!

In a medium-sized pot, combine the water, Old Bay seasoning, Cajun Spice, halved lemons, bay leaves, parsley, beer, onion, garlic, and hot sauce. Bring the pot to a boil, and let it continue to boil for 5 to 10 minutes, letting all the ingredients cook together.

If you're serving the shrimp hot, then get your remoulade sauce ready.

When the water is boiling, add the shrimp. Stir them with a pair of tongs and cook for 3 to 5 minutes. To test doneness, look at where the heads would be, and when they're opaque all the way through, they're ready. If you're serving the shrimp hot, strain them before putting them on a platter.

If you're serving the shrimp cold, don't rinse them when they're done cooking. Just strain them, spread them on a sheet pan, and refrigerate until cold.

I also like to sprinkle Old Bay and Cajun seasoning on the shrimp once they're on the platter. If you're serving them hot, serve with melted butter. With either hot or cold shrimp, serve with the Red Remoulade, lemon quarters, and reserved parsley sprigs.

HAWAIIAN-STYLE TUNA POKE

with Baked Wonton Chips

SERVES 4

PICKLED BEAN SPROUTS

½ lb (226 g) bean sprouts

½ cup (120 ml) lemon juice

½ tbsp (3 g) minced ginger

2 tsp (10 g) minced garlic

2 tsp (10 g) chili-garlic sambal paste

2 tbsp (30 ml) soy sauce

1 tbsp (18 g) salt

1 cup (240 ml) hot water

POKE DRESSING

2 tbsp (12 g) minced green onion

1 tbsp (6 g) peeled and minced fresh ginger

1 tbsp (10 g) minced onion

1 tbsp (6 g) minced jalapeño

1 tbsp (15 g) minced garlic

2 tbsp (30 ml) soy sauce

2 tbsp (30 ml) rice wine vinegar

2 tbsp (30 ml) sesame oil

4 tbsp (60 ml) olive oil

½ tsp chili flakes

½ tsp sugar

12 wonton wrappers, thawed if frozen

Salt, to taste

1 lb (454 g) ahi tuna, diced small

¼ cup (24 g) minced green onion

2 tbsp (6 g) dried hijiki seaweed, reconstituted in water, optional

¼ cup (31 g) macadamia nuts, lightly crushed, for garnish

Cilantro sprigs, for garnish

I ate tuna poke (pronounced po-kay) for the first time at Ken Oringer's now-closed Boston restaurant, Clio, about 20-plus years ago. It was so amazing that I tried to duplicate it, and I ran my version as a special one night when I was the chef at Tremont 647 in Boston's South End. After that, I served it for over a decade. The key is to keep everything cold. It's so good, it's like tuna on steroids.

Make the pickled bean sprouts: Mix all ingredients together and set aside. Alternatively, pickled bean sprouts are available at specialty food stores.

Make the poke dressing: Mix all ingredients together and set aside.

Make the baked wonton chips: Preheat the oven to 350°F (177°C) and spray a baking sheet with nonstick spray. Slice each wonton wrapper in half diagonally to make two triangles, and place them in a single layer on the baking sheet. Sprinkle with salt to taste. Bake for 5 to 7 minutes, or until crisp and golden.

The wonton chips will keep for a week or so in an airtight container. To re-crisp and reheat before serving, bake them in the oven for about 4 minutes.

Mix the tuna, pickled bean sprouts, green onion, and seaweed (optional) together, dress with 2 to 4 oz (57 to 114 ml) of the poke dressing, and place on a plate. Garnish with crushed macadamia nuts and cilantro sprigs and serve with the wonton chips.

BLUE CRAB EMPANADAS

MASA DOUGH
1½ cups (174 g) masa harina flour

½ tbsp (6 g) Sazón Goya® with annatto

1 tsp salt

2 cups (480 ml) water

1 tbsp (15 ml) blended oil

EMPANADA FILLING
1 lb (454 g) blue crab meat

¾ cup (174 g) mascarpone

1 shallot, minced

1 tbsp (4 g) minced cilantro

½ tsp ground cumin

S&P Mix (page 133), to taste

Canola oil, for frying

Lime wedges, for serving

Hot sauce, for serving

Think of these empanadas as a combination of all your favorite things jammed into a little pocket of love. It's as if a New England crab cake met a Chinese rangoon and they moved to South America together. You can easily buy the wrappers in your frozen food section, and those are just fine. But: If you take the time to make the dough in this recipe, you won't regret it. It's absolutely my favorite part. I swear, you could wrap your socks in it and fry it, and it would be utterly delicious.

Prepare the dough: Place the masa harina flour in a large bowl. Add the Sazón Goya and salt. Stir to mix well. Add the water and oil and mix to form a dough. Pat the dough into a ball and knead for 2 minutes or until smooth. Cover with plastic and set aside for 20 minutes.

Make the filling: Combine all ingredients well and season with S&P Mix.

Make the empanadas: Break off walnut-sized portions of the dough, about 2½ tablespoons (50 g) for each one, and form each portion into a ball by rolling it between the palms of your hands. Place the balls of dough between two pieces of oiled parchment paper or plastic wrap, roll or press each out to form very thin circles. Remove the top plastic and place 2 tablespoons (30 g) of the filling in the center of each. Then, using the plastic underneath, fold the dough over to enclose the filling, forming a half circle. Tightly seal the edges by crimping them with the tines of a fork.

Fill a large pot with canola oil and heat over medium heat to 350°F (177°C).

Carefully place three or four empanadas at a time in the heated oil and fry for about 4 minutes until golden on all sides. Using a slotted spoon, transfer the empanadas to a plate lined with paper towels. Serve with lime wedges and your favorite hot sauce.

JALAPEÑO, CHEDDAR, AND BACON HUSH PUPPIES

I'll tell you, I've had a lot more bad hush puppies than good ones in my lifetime. Usually they're super dense and relatively flavorless. Not these babies: They're light, fluffy, and full of flavor. God, I love these things.

4 cups (500 g) all-purpose flour

1 cup (122 g) cornmeal

4 tsp (18 g) baking powder

¾ cup (150 g) sugar

2 tsp (12 g) salt

½ tsp baking soda

¼ cup (28 g) onion powder

1 tbsp (7 g) Cajun Spice (page 137)

1 cup (112 g) bacon bits

1½ cups (170 g) grated yellow Cheddar

3 cups (720 ml) milk

3 eggs

¼ cup (60 ml) apple cider vinegar

¾ cup (120 g) canned diced pickled jalapeños

Canola oil, for frying

S&P Mix (page 133), to taste

Spicy Creole Ranch Dressing (page 141) or Red Remoulade (page 145), for serving

In a large bowl, mix the flour, cornmeal, baking powder, sugar, salt, baking soda, onion powder, and Cajun Spice; this is the dry mixture.

In a small bowl, mix the bacon bits, Cheddar, milk, eggs, vinegar, and jalapeños; this is the wet mix. The vinegar will curdle the milk a little, which is fine.

Add the wet ingredients to the dry mixture all at once, and stir until just blended. In a pot, heat canola oil to about 350°F (177°C). Using a small scoop, place a scoop of the batter into the oil and fry until golden brown and cooked through. Season with S&P Mix to taste and serve these with either Spicy Creole Ranch Dressing or Red Remoulade.

BEST EVAH CLAM CHOWDER

with Black Pepper Bacon Bits and Smoked Oyster Crackers

SMOKED OYSTER CRACKERS

¼ tsp liquid smoke

Smoked salt

2 tbsp (28 g) butter, melted

2 cups (90 g) oyster crackers

4 tbsp (57 g) butter

½ cup (115 g) minced raw bacon

¼ cup (25 g) diced celery

¼ cup (32 g) diced carrot

¼ cup (40 g) diced onion

¼ cup (22 g) diced fennel

1 tsp fresh thyme leaves

2 bay leaves

¼ cup (31 g) all-purpose flour

2½ cups (600 ml) clam juice

2 cups (364 g) diced clam meat

½ lb (226 g) Idaho potatoes, peeled, diced, and boiled separately until just cooked through

2 tbsp (8 g) finely chopped parsley leaves

4 tbsp (12 g) minced fresh chives, divided

1–2 cups (240–480 ml) heavy cream

S&P Mix (page 133), to taste

¼ cup (28 g) Black Pepper Bacon Bits (page 138)

This dish is as Boston as it gets. Everybody serves a version of this in downtown Boston, I assure you. This version, however, is the best I've ever had. I like that it has carrots and fennel in it, which you rarely see. I also really dig the creative garnishes—the oyster crackers are smoky, and the bacon is deliciously peppery and full of flavor. Okay, now I'm hungry.

Make the smoked oyster crackers: Preheat the oven to 350°F (177°C). Mix the liquid smoke, salt, and butter in a small pot and melt. Place the crackers in a medium-sized bowl, pour the butter mixture over the crackers, and toss until all crackers are coated. Spread on a sheet pan and bake for 4 to 6 minutes. Remove from the oven and allow to cool. Store in an airtight container at room temperature.

In a pot over medium heat, melt the butter. Add the bacon and cook until it begins to crisp, about 10 minutes. Add the celery, carrot, onion, fennel, thyme, and bay leaves and sauté until the vegetables soften, about 6 minutes. Stir in the flour and cook for 2 minutes—do not allow the flour to brown. Gradually whisk in the clam juice. Add the clam meat and potatoes and simmer everything for 10 to 15 minutes to blend the flavors, stirring frequently. Finish with the parsley and 2 tablespoons (6 g) of chives. Cool the chowder base until ready to use.

When you are ready to use it, heat the chowder base with enough heavy cream to reach your desired consistency and season with the S&P Mix, if necessary. Remove the bay leaves. Garnish with Black Pepper Bacon Bits, half of the smoked oyster crackers (reserve the rest for later use), and the remaining 2 tablespoons (6 g) of minced chives.

CHIPOTLE BUTTERNUT SQUASH BISQUE

with Cinnamon Croutons and Bourbon Whipped Cream

SERVES 4-6

You know something is good when you read a recipe that screams fall but you are willing to make it in the dead of summer. This is one of those. These flavor combinations are the best: slightly spicy, creamy, crunchy, savory all in one bite! Now let's go swimming or skiing.

BUTTERNUT BISQUE

¼ lb (113 g) butter

2 tbsp (30 ml) extra virgin olive oil

4 shallots, sliced

2½ lb (1.1 kg) butternut squash, peeled and diced

2–4 canned chipotle peppers in adobo sauce (depending on how hot you like it)

4 cups (960 ml) chicken or vegetable stock

½ cup (120 ml) maple syrup

½ cup (110 g) light brown sugar

1 tsp cinnamon

½ tsp nutmeg

1½ cups (360 ml) heavy cream

Salt, to taste

White pepper, to taste

CINNAMON CROUTONS

4 slices cinnamon bread (brioche or monkey bread works best), cut into very small cubes

2 tbsp (28 g) butter, browned in a small saucepan over medium heat

1 tsp sugar

¼ tsp cinnamon

BOURBON WHIPPED CREAM

2 cups (480 ml) heavy cream

1 tbsp (15 g) sugar

2 tbsp (30 ml) bourbon

2 tbsp (6 g) minced chives, for garnish

Make the bisque: Melt the butter with the olive oil in a heavy-bottomed saucepan over medium heat. Add the shallots and sweat until softened, but don't allow them to color. Add the butternut squash, chipotle peppers, stock, maple syrup, brown sugar, cinnamon, and nutmeg, and simmer until soft, about 20 minutes. Remove from heat and then purée in a blender until smooth. Add heavy cream and season with salt and white pepper to taste.

Make the croutons: Preheat the oven to 375°F (191°C). Toss the bread in the brown butter, sugar, and cinnamon. Bake on a sheet pan for 5 to 6 minutes until golden. Remove and set aside until the soup is finished.

Make the bourbon whipped cream: Add the heavy cream and sugar to a chilled bowl and beat until soft peaks form, about 3 minutes. Add bourbon gradually while beating on low, until the cream is stiff but not over-whipped.

Divide the soup among bowls and place a few croutons in the middle of each. Place a dollop of whipped cream on top of the croutons—that will help slow down its melting. Garnish with chives and serve.

RECORD TIME

There are dishes out there that take days and days to make and are better off for it. (If you've ever had truly great ramen, you know what I'm talking about.) But is that really what we all need to do every day in order to eat delicious meals? Absolutely no way! These quick-as-can-be recipes are the antidote to all that—whether it's a luxurious swordfish in fragrant, sweet chimichurri (page 28) or a substantial Caesar salad (page 27) that'll knock your socks off. This chapter proves you don't need to be stuck in your kitchen forever to easily whip up some fantastic food.

BABY KALE CAESAR

with Crispy Soft-Boiled Eggs, Asiago, and Pickled Onions

SERVES 2

2 tbsp (28 g) butter

1 clove garlic, minced

3 slices French bread, cubed

4–6 cups (170–255 g) baby kale

Sour Cream Caesar Dressing (page 165), to taste

2 Crispy Soft-Boiled Eggs (page 169)

¼ cup (80 g) Pickled Red Onions (page 162)

¼ cup (30 g) shaved asiago cheese

I've been a huge fan of Caesar salads for as long as I can remember. I order them constantly at restaurants, and I love checking out different variations when I come across them. Truly, the salad never gets old to me. As for this one, well, it's a stunner! When you cut open that crispy, absolutely delicious egg and it runs all over the salad? That's one of the best eating moments out there.

Make the croutons: Preheat the oven to 350°F (177°C). In a large sauté pan, melt the butter over medium heat. Stir in the garlic and stir for about a minute. Add the bread cubes and toss to coat. Spread evenly on a baking sheet and bake for 5 to 7 minutes, or until crisp and dry. Check frequently to prevent burning. Let them cool.

Toss the baby kale in the Caesar dressing and divide between two plates. Top with one crispy soft-boiled egg on each plate, plus the pickled onions, croutons, and shaved asiago.

SWORDFISH

with Golden Raisins and Calabrian Chili Chimichurri

2 lb (907 g) swordfish, cut into 4 steaks

S&P Mix (page 133), to taste

1 lemon, cut into wedges

2 tbsp (6 g) chopped fresh oregano

¼ cup plus 2 tbsp (90 ml) extra virgin olive oil, divided

¼ cup (40 g) golden raisins

½ cup (120 ml) boiling water

½ cup (120 ml) Calabrian Chili Chimichurri (page 157), divided

½ cup (75 g) cherry tomatoes, for serving

See? I told you that my Calabrian Chili Chimichurri (page 157) makes just about anything sing. And as this dish proves, that's especially true of swordfish. But add the mild sweetness of golden raisins to the meatiness of the swordfish, along with the acidic tartness and bright flavors of the chimichurri, and all come shining through.

Place the swordfish steaks in a nonreactive baking dish. Season on both sides with S&P Mix to taste. Squeeze the lemon wedges over them, discarding any seeds that fall out. Sprinkle with oregano, drizzle with ¼ cup (60 ml) of olive oil, and let marinate for 25 to 30 minutes.

Place the raisins in a medium heat-proof bowl. Pour the boiling water over them and let the raisins soak for 15 minutes.

Spoon 4 tablespoons (60 ml) of the chimichurri on the swordfish steaks, using the back of a spoon to coat, and spread it all over.

Drain the raisins and add them to the remaining 4 tablespoons (60 ml) of the chimichurri and mix.

Heat a large pan over medium heat and add 2 tablespoons (30 ml) of olive oil. When the oil is just hot, cook the swordfish steaks and the cherry tomatoes together, until the fish is browned and sizzling on one side, about 5 minutes. Carefully flip the fish steaks over. Cook about 5 minutes longer, until the fish is just cooked through and the tomatoes are soft and wilting or bursting.

Serve the swordfish steaks topped with the tomatoes and a big dollop of the remaining chimichurri.

CHRISTINA'S ROMAINE HEART SALAD

with Rajas, Chipotle-Horseradish Dressing, and Jalapeño Cornbread Croutons

CHIPOTLE-HORSERADISH DRESSING
¼ cup (60 ml) mayonnaise

2 tbsp (30 g) prepared horseradish

2 tsp (11 g) minced chipotle peppers in adobo sauce

½ tsp lemon zest

S&P Mix (page 133), to taste

RAJAS
½ poblano pepper

½ red bell pepper

1 tbsp (15 ml) extra virgin olive oil

½ small onion, julienned

S&P Mix (page 133), to taste

JALAPEÑO CORNBREAD CROUTONS
2 tbsp (28 g) butter

1 jalapeño, diced small

1 clove garlic, minced

1 cup (36 g) small diced cooked cornbread (any bread would also work)

S&P Mix (page 133), to taste

ASSEMBLY
1 head of romaine lettuce, outer leaves removed and split into 4 pieces

2 tbsp (15 g) cotija cheese, crumbled, for garnish

Christina Wilson is a good friend, and together we are the two sous-chefs on *Hell's Kitchen*. She was also the winner of season 10 on the show, and now oversees all of Gordon Ramsay's restaurants in North America. (So, in case there's any doubt, she's a complete badass in the kitchen.) This is her recipe, and she was gracious enough to share it with me, so now I'm sharing it with you. If you know what's good for you, you will make this right now, you donkey!

Make the chipotle horseradish dressing: Combine all the ingredients and season to taste.

Make the rajas: Place the poblano and bell pepper on a grill, turning occasionally until the skins are completely charred, about 5 minutes if your grill is hot enough. Allow them to cool slightly, peel off the skins, cut the peppers into thin strips, and remove the seeds. In a large sauté pan, heat the olive oil and add the onion. Cook slowly over medium-low heat, stirring occasionally until slightly caramelized, 10 to 15 minutes. Combine with the pepper strips and season with S&P Mix to taste.

Make the jalapeño cornbread croutons: Preheat the oven to 350°F (177°C). In a small pan, melt the butter, add the jalapeño and garlic, and cook until soft, about 5 minutes. Place the butter mixture in a mixing bowl, add the cornbread, and toss to coat. Season with S&P Mix to taste. Transfer the cornbread to a baking sheet and bake for 5 to 7 minutes to your desired crunchiness.

To assemble, divide the romaine equally on two plates. Drizzle with the dressing and scatter with the rajas. Garnish with the croutons and cotija cheese.

WARM DILLY BEANS

1 tbsp (18 g) salt, plus more for boiling, divided

½ lb (226 g) wax beans (or green beans, or a mix), trimmed and cleaned

1 cup (240 ml) white vinegar

1 tbsp (15 g) sugar

2 tbsp (30 ml) extra virgin olive oil

2 tbsp (30 g) sliced garlic

1 tbsp (10 g) sliced shallot

¼ tsp chili flakes

½ tsp coriander seed, crushed

1 tbsp (3 g) minced scallion

1½ tbsp (5 g) chopped dill

This is an outstanding side dish. It is so unique and more than delivers on flavor. Dilly beans are generally just a pickled green bean in the South, but preparing them the way I describe imparts less of a pickled taste and more flavor. (The dill is my favorite part, just in case you were wondering.)

Salt a large pot of water, about 2 tablespoons (36 g) of salt per quart (960 ml) of water. Bring to a boil over high heat and blanch the beans for 2 to 3 minutes, then plunge them in a bowl of ice water to stop the cooking. Drain and put them into a large bowl.

In a separate pot, bring the vinegar, sugar, and 1 tablespoon (18 g) of salt to a boil and pour over the green beans. Let sit for at least an hour, the longer the better. You now have pickled beans, which will keep forever in the refrigerator. (And, by the way, they're a perfect garnish for Bloody Marys.)

In a large pan over medium heat, add the olive oil, garlic, and shallot and sweat until translucent. Add the chili flakes and coriander seed and toast briefly. Drain the beans and add them to the pan. Once warm, add the scallion and dill and toss. Serve warm. (Although frankly, they're pretty good cold, too.)

SHRIMP AND OLIVE ORECCHIETTE

Pinch of salt

1 lb (454 g) orecchiette pasta

¾ lb (340 g) medium-sized raw shrimp, deveined, shells and tails removed

½ cup (120 ml) extra virgin olive oil

1 tsp chopped garlic

1¼ cups (300 g) Castelvetrano olives, pitted and chopped

1 cup (117 g) small-chopped walnuts

S&P Mix (page 133), to taste

¼ cup (38 g) feta, crumbled

1 lemon, zested and sliced into wedges with seeds removed

¼ cup (15 g) chopped fresh parsley

The flavor-to-effort ratio on this easy weeknight dinner is off the charts. From start to finish, it takes about 25 minutes, and it punches far above its weight class on taste, thanks to the fruity Castelvetrano olives mixed with earthy walnuts and sweet, briny shrimp. It's rich and fresh tasting, which makes it a no-brainer to whip up through the entire year.

In a large pot of water, add a pinch of salt and heat over high heat until boiling. Add the orecchiette and wait about 1 minute, then add the shrimp. By the time the pasta is al dente, or cooked through but still slightly chewy, the shrimp will have turned pink. Scoop out a cup (240 ml) of the pasta water and set aside, then drain the pasta and shrimp together.

Meanwhile, in a large pot, mix the olive oil, garlic, olives, and walnuts over medium heat. Stir occasionally for about 5 minutes. Season with S&P Mix to taste.

Add half of the reserved pasta water to the olive mixture and continue stirring until everything is combined. If the sauce seems too thick, add a tablespoon (15 ml) more of pasta water. Add the orecchiette and shrimp, then the feta, still stirring. Add half the lemon zest and squeeze lemon wedges over top. Check the seasoning and adjust with S&P Mix to taste. Serve on four individual plates, topped with parsley and the remaining lemon zest.

– THE –
CHICKEN CHANNEL

I've basically made a career out of selling chicken. And that's not just because people crave it that much (although frankly, yeah—they do), but also because I love it so much myself that I always want to make it as irresistible as I possibly can. So this chapter's dedicated to The Chicken . . . that versatile and scrumptious bird in all its glory, with an eye toward what we humans can do in the kitchen to make it taste beyond magical when we set our minds to it. Best of all, these recipes (like all the others in this book) are pretty simple; they just use a few twists and turns to coax the best and most interesting flavors and textures out of the honorable bird. Love the chicken, and the chicken will love you back, I say.

CAJUN ROTISSERIE CHICKEN DIP

8 tbsp (116 g) cream cheese, softened

8 tbsp (116 g) mascarpone cheese

1 cup (240 ml) Spicy Creole Ranch Dressing (page 141)

¼ cup (28 g) shredded mozzarella

¼ cup (28 g) shredded pepper jack

3 cups (375) shredded rotisserie chicken, skin removed

¼ cup (34 g) your favorite blue cheese, for garnish

½ tsp Cajun Spice (page 137), for garnish

2 tbsp (6 g) minced chives, for garnish

This recipe has been in every publication in Boston. My publicist said she would never let the dish die because it is just that good. I love it because it's super easy to make, it's unbelievably delicious, and it's a touch different from your usual dip, thanks to the Cajun twist.

P.S. You know you have a rotisserie chicken in your fridge as we speak!

Preheat the oven to 350°F (177°C).

In a medium bowl, whisk the cream cheese and mascarpone until smooth. Stir in the Spicy Creole Ranch Dressing, mozzarella, and pepper jack. Fold in the chicken, pour the mixture into a cast iron pan, and bake for 20 minutes, or until the chicken mixture is hot and bubbling.

Garnish with crumbled blue cheese, a dusting of the Cajun Spice, and fresh chopped chives. Serve immediately and with anything . . . crudités, pita bread, tortilla chips, grilled bread, or do what I do and put it in a grilled cheese (see next book).

SPICY GRILLED CHICKEN WINGS

with Scallion Sour Cream and Shiitake Mushroom Relish

SERVES 6

This recipe is a perfect example of why I'm so crazy about chicken. You take a too-often-overlooked piece of the bird, like a wing, and it's so easy to make it into a masterpiece. I love the wing. I am one with the wing. I respect the wing. And after you make this recipe, you'll be the same way—I guarantee it.

GRILLED WINGS

2 cups (480 ml) soy sauce

1 cup (240 ml) Dijon mustard

1 cup (240 ml) chicken broth

¾ cup (180 ml) Tabasco sauce

¼ cup (60 g) chopped garlic

2 tbsp (8 g) chopped parsley

24 chicken wings

SCALLION SOUR CREAM

½ cup (120 ml) sour cream

2 tbsp (30 ml) buttermilk

1 tbsp (6 g) finely minced scallion

S&P Mix (page 133), to taste

SHIITAKE MUSHROOM RELISH

¾ lb (340 g) shiitake mushrooms, stems removed

2 tbsp (30 ml) extra virgin olive oil, divided

S&P Mix (page 133), to taste, divided

2 tsp (6 g) minced onion

2 cloves garlic, minced

1 tsp chopped parsley

1 tsp chopped sage

1 tsp chopped rosemary

½ tsp chopped thyme

1 tbsp (15 ml) balsamic vinegar

2 tsp (10 ml) lemon juice

Marinate the wings: Mix the soy sauce, mustard, chicken broth, Tabasco sauce, garlic, and parsley together. Reserve ¼ cup (60 ml) of the marinade and set it aside. Pour the rest over the chicken wings, making sure all of the wings are submerged. Cover and refrigerate, letting the wings sit a minimum of 24 hours (but honestly, they are far more flavorful if you let them sit for 48 hours).

Make the scallion sour cream: Whisk all ingredients together and season with S&P Mix to taste.

Make the shiitake mushroom relish: Preheat the oven to 400°F (204°C). Toss the mushrooms with 1 tablespoon (15 ml) of the olive oil and season with S&P Mix to taste. Roast on a baking pan for about 20 minutes. Once cooked, slice the mushrooms carefully while still hot and then toss them in a bowl with the onion, garlic, parsley, sage, rosemary, thyme, the remaining tablespoon (15 ml) of olive oil, vinegar, and lemon juice. Season with more S&P Mix to taste.

Preheat a grill to high heat and remove the wings from the marinade, discarding the liquid. Grill the wings for about 15 minutes, turning each one often so they don't burn. Heat up the reserved marinade in a small saucepan. Smear the scallion sour cream on the bottom of a plate, then place the grilled chicken wings on top. Drizzle some of the warm marinade over them and garnish with the shiitake mushroom relish. Serve immediately.

HOT HONEY CHICKEN MAC 'N' CHEESE

with Crunchy Parmesan Panko

MAKES 4 GOOD-SIZED PORTIONS

CHEESE SAUCE
2 tbsp (28 g) butter
1 cup (240 ml) half-and-half
¾ lb (340 g) yellow American cheese, shredded
¼ cup (28 g) shredded pepper jack cheese
¼ cups (28 g) shredded Cheddar cheese
2 tsp (10 ml) Dijon mustard
½ tsp chili powder
½ tsp paprika
1 tbsp (15 ml) Worcestershire sauce
1 tbsp (15 ml) Crystal hot sauce
S&P Mix (page 133), to taste

CAMPANELLE PASTA
½ lb (226 g) campanelle pasta
Salt, for boiling

HOT HONEY CHICKEN
2 tbsp (30 ml) canola oil
2 lb (907 g) chicken breast, diced
1 tbsp (9 g) Hot Chicken Spice Rub (page 150)
2 tbsp (30 ml) Buttermilk's Hot Honey (page 161)
S&P Mix (page 133), to taste

CRUNCHY PARMESAN PANKO
½ cup (28 g) panko breadcrumbs, lightly toasted
¼ cup (25 g) shredded Parmesan cheese
2 tbsp (28 g) butter, melted
1 tbsp (4 g) minced parsley
1 tbsp (3 g) minced chives
S&P Mix (page 133), to taste

There's just so much I have to say about mac 'n' cheese, there isn't enough ink in the world to write it all. And sure, there are a lot of bad versions out there, but this one is straight-up killer—and with its touch of honey, it isn't the kind of thing you taste every day. Bottom line: It's crunchy, creamy, and spicy-sweet all in one bite. Lights-out good!

Make the cheese sauce: Place all the ingredients in a bowl over a pot of simmering water (aka double boiler) and continue to whisk until everything is melted together and very smooth. Season with S&P Mix.

Make the pasta: Cook the pasta in salted boiling water until al dente according to package directions. Drain.

Make the hot honey chicken: In a large saucepan over high heat, add the canola oil and cook until hot. Add the chicken breast and cook until browned and about 75 percent of the way cooked, for 6 to 7 minutes. Add the Hot Chicken Spice Rub and reduce the heat to medium so as not to burn the spices. Once the chicken is finished cooking, shut off the heat, toss with Buttermilk's Hot Honey, and season with S&P Mix. Set aside.

Make the crunchy Parmesan panko: Mix all the ingredients together in a medium-sized bowl.

Once the pasta is cooked, toss liberally with the cheese sauce, then place the mac 'n' cheese mixture in serving bowls. Top with the chicken and crispy Parmesan panko. Serve immediately.

CHICKEN, MUSHROOM, AND GOAT CHEESE QUESADILLAS

with Avocado-Tomatillo Salsa

MAKES 8 QUESADILLAS

TOMATILLO SALSA
6 fresh tomatillos, husked, rinsed, and halved

1 avocado

1 tbsp (6 g) roughly chopped jalapeño

1 clove garlic

½ cup (8 g) cilantro leaves

2 tbsp (30 ml) lime juice

1 tbsp (15 ml) orange juice

S&P Mix (page 133), to taste

QUESADILLA FILLING
1 tbsp (15 ml) extra virgin olive oil

1 lb (454 g) mixed wild mushrooms, sliced

2 cloves garlic, minced

¼ cup (40 g) small-diced onion

1 (10-oz [283-g]) bag fresh baby spinach

2 cups (250 g) shredded rotisserie chicken

S&P Mix (page 133), to taste

½ cup (56 g) shredded pepper jack cheese

1 cup (112 g) crumbled goat cheese

¼ cup (15 g) roughly chopped cilantro

½ tsp ground cumin

½ tsp chili powder

QUESADILLAS
8 (6" [15-cm]) corn tortillas

2 tbsp (30 ml) extra virgin olive oil

1 packet chili seasoning or your favorite Latin spice

Cilantro sprigs, for garnish

2 limes, cut into wedges

In my humble opinion, there's nothing worse than someone trying to pass off a quesadilla as some melted cheese in a flacid, flavorless flour tortilla. Those days are gone, mis amigos! This is the most flavorful, crunchiest, deliciously textured, gloriously colorful, and most properly made quesadilla this side of the Rio Grande.

Make the tomatillo salsa: Place the tomatillos into a food processor or blender. Add the avocado, jalapeño, garlic, cilantro, lime juice, and orange juice. Season with S&P Mix to taste. Process until smooth; adjust the seasoning as needed. Transfer to a serving bowl.

Make the quesadilla filling: Start with a large sauté pan over high heat and add the olive oil. Then add the mushrooms and cook until nicely browned, for 8 to 10 minutes. Add the garlic and onion and cook until soft. Add the spinach and shredded chicken and cook until just warm. Season with S&P Mix. Remove from the heat and cool until the mixture is at room temperature. Mix the pepper jack, goat cheese, cilantro, cumin, and chili powder together. Combine with the spinach and mushroom mix.

Make the quesadillas: Take about ¼ cup (40 g) of the filling and place on one corn tortilla, then fold the tortilla over and continue until all are made. Brush the quesadillas liberally with the olive oil on both sides, then sprinkle chili seasoning on each side.

To cook the quesadillas, either use a nonstick electric griddle or a large nonstick pan over medium heat. Place the quesadillas on the griddle or in the pan and cook until golden brown and crispy on both sides, for 3 to 5 minutes. Don't worry about the mixture falling out—if it does, it will caramelize and make the quesadillas even better!

Serve with the tomatillo salsa and garnish with cilantro and lime wedges.

ROTISSERIE CHICKEN AND YUKON GOLD POTATO CAKES

with Sunny-Side Up Eggs and Chipotle Hollandaise

4 tbsp (57 g) butter, divided

¼ cup (58 g) small-diced bacon

½ cup (80 g) diced onion

½ cup (50 g) diced celery

½ cup (55 g) green bell pepper

½ cup (55 g) red bell pepper

1 jalapeño, seeded and minced

2 cloves garlic cloves

1 rotisserie chicken, meat picked and shredded (about 1 lb [454 g] of meat)

1 tbsp (7 g) smoked paprika

½ tsp dried thyme or 1 tbsp (2 g) minced fresh thyme

S&P Mix (page 133), to taste

People love these suckers. Hell, I've eaten a warm one in my car before I even got home. This recipe is a great idea for using leftover (or yes, even a freshly bought) chicken. The potato cake is delicious, has a ton of flavor, and makes a killer brunch. Feel free to swap out the chicken for another protein, too—shredded beef, pork, or even crabmeat all work extremely well.

In a large cast iron pan, heat 2 tablespoons (28 g) of the butter over medium heat until hot. Add the bacon and cook until the fat has rendered and the meat is starting to crisp up. Add the onion, celery, green pepper, red pepper, jalapeño, and garlic and sauté until soft, for 3 to 5 minutes. Toss in the chicken meat, paprika, and thyme and cook for 2 to 3 minutes, or until the chicken is warm. Season with S&P Mix. Transfer the mixture to a mixing bowl and let cool to room temperature.

(continued)

9 medium Yukon gold potatoes, cooked until just soft

3 tbsp (18 g) minced green onions

3 tbsp (45 ml) canola oil

¼ cup (31 g) cornmeal

6 eggs

Chipotle Hollandaise Sauce (page 142)

2 tbsp (6 g) minced chives, for garnish

Fresh cracked pepper, for garnish

Crush the potatoes with your hands and add them to the mixing bowl with the green onions. Season with S&P Mix. Form into six cakes about the size of a hockey puck and chill until cold. When ready to cook, clean out the cast iron pan, place over medium heat, and add the canola oil. Dust the cakes with cornmeal and place them in the pan. Sear well on each side and either turn down the heat and cook until warm or place in a 350°F (177°C) oven for about 10 minutes. Season with S&P Mix and keep warm.

Make the sunny-side up eggs: Add the remaining 2 tablespoons (28 g) of butter to a medium-sized nonstick pan over medium-low heat. When the butter is just hot, crack 3 eggs into the pan (there will be two batches of eggs to cook). Once the edges of the eggs begin to turn white, use a small spoon to carefully spoon the hot butter over the whites of the eggs, avoiding the yolk. After 1 to 2 minutes of cooking, the whites will set. Remove the eggs from the pan with a slotted spatula, then place them on a cutting board and, using a ring mold, cut out a perfectly round egg.

To build each plate, place a potato cake in the center of the plate and top with one sunny-side up egg, then spoon Chipotle Hollandaise Sauce around the cake. Garnish with the chives and fresh cracked pepper.

BEER-BATTERED CHICKEN SANDWICH

with Creamy Chipotle Coleslaw and Dill Pickles

CHICKEN SANDWICH

Canola oil, for frying

2 tbsp (16 g) self-rising flour

6 boneless chicken thighs (breasts work as well, but thighs are superior)

6 brioche hamburger buns

4 tbsp (57 g) butter, melted

24-ish dill pickle chips

BEER BATTER

2 cups (250 g) self-rising flour

3 tbsp (30 g) rice flour

1 tsp baking powder

1 tbsp (6 g) lemon pepper

1 tsp curry powder

1 tsp salt

1½ cups (360 ml) soda water

1 (12-oz [355-ml]) bottle beer (preferably Lager)

Okay, I know y'all don't love to fry in your home. It makes a mess, they say. It's difficult. It's oily, etc., etc. Blah, blah, blah. Well, I promise if you do this right, you won't regret it for a second, because it's the best thing ever. This is the batter we use at all my restaurants—for everything from chicken and fish to shrimp and Oreo cookies. (Yes, that's right.) It's an excellent (and one might even argue crucial) batter to have in your repertoire. What's the saying? "Give a man a fish and he eats for a day. Teach a man to fish and he eats for a lifetime." Well, go fish. Because this batter recipe is for life.

Prepare to make the chicken: In a deep fryer or large Dutch oven, heat about 4 inches (10 cm) of canola oil over high heat, to about 330°F (166°C).

Make the beer batter: Mix together the self-rising flour, rice flour, baking powder, lemon pepper, curry powder, salt, soda water, and beer in a bowl.

Prepare the chicken: Dust the flour over the chicken thighs on each side. Dip each piece of chicken in the beer batter and shake, letting excess batter fall off. Carefully place the chicken in the hot oil (you may need to fry in batches, depending on your pan size) and fry for 10 to 12 minutes, or until golden brown and the juices run clear. You can also use a meat thermometer and make sure it registers to 165°F (74°C) for the internal temperature.

(continued)

CREAMY CHIPOTLE COLESLAW

¼ cup (60 ml) mayonnaise

½ cup (120 ml) white vinegar

3 tbsp (38 g) sugar

1 tsp celery seed

1 tbsp (17 g) minced chipotle peppers in adobo sauce

S&P Mix (page 133), to taste

6 cups (534 g) thinly sliced green or Napa cabbage

½ red onion, julienned thin

⅔ cup (73 g) shredded carrot

2 tbsp (8 g) chopped flat-leaf parsley

Make the coleslaw: In a large bowl, combine the mayonnaise, vinegar, sugar, celery seed, chipotle, and season with S&P Mix to taste. Add the cabbage, onion, carrot, and parsley to the bowl and toss to coat. Serve immediately if you like it super crispy, but it will also keep a couples of days if you like it on the softer side. Makes about 6 cups (880 g).

To assemble the sandwich, brush the insides of the buns with butter and griddle in a frying pan or on a skillet until warm and toasted. Top the chicken with the slaw and pickles, and serve on the brioche buns.

PRIME TIME RECIPES

Some people share recipes from their favorite barbecues, from their most memorable birthday parties, or from their grandma. (I do that too, actually, on page 75.) But what I get asked for a lot is recipes I've whipped up on various TV cooking shows, and frankly, I'm happy to share. And not just because you bought my book (although that helps), but because when it comes to sharing good food, my philosophy is: The more, the merrier. Enjoy!

PAN-SEARED SEA SCALLOPS

with Apple Purée, Chive Mayo, and Candied Walnut Salad

SERVES 4

FRESH APPLE PURÉE
2 Granny Smith apples, peeled and diced
¾ cup (180 ml) apple juice
2 tbsp (25 g) sugar
2 tbsp (30 ml) apple cider vinegar
Pinch of salt

CHIVE MAYO
¼ cup (60 ml) mayonnaise
1 tbsp (15 ml) apple cider vinegar
2 tbsp (6 g) finely minced or puréed chives
Pinch of salt

CANDIED WALNUT SALAD
¼ cup (28 g) candied walnuts (or any other candied nut you see at the store)
¼ apple, peeled and julienned
1 tbsp (6 g) small-diced celery
1 tbsp (2 g) celery leaves
A few fresh parsley leaves
1 tsp extra virgin olive oil
¼ tsp lemon juice or ½ tsp any store-bought vinaigrette
Pinch of salt

SEARED SEA SCALLOPS
Canola oil
16 10/20 dry sea scallops
Salt
Curry powder
Fresh herb leaves, for garnish

This is one of the signature dishes of *Hell's Kitchen*. The contestants seem to mess this up a lot, but I'm going to teach you how to make scallops calmly and do Gordon Ramsay proud. This is among the most stunning plates of food in this book. The best part is it looks and reads fancy, and will definitely impress everyone, but it's basically scallops, apple sauce, and nuts.

Make the apple purée: Place all the ingredients in a small pot and simmer on low heat until the apples are very soft, about 15 minutes. Strain and reserve the liquid. Purée the apples until smooth, adding in the reserved liquid as needed until it's very smooth and the consistency of apple sauce. Let it cool, then place it in a squeeze bottle. (Or . . . just buy apple sauce and use that. Nobody will know.)

For the chive mayo, mix the mayonnaise, apple cider vinegar, and chives in a bowl and season with a pinch of salt. Place in a squeeze bottle and set aside.

For the candied walnut salad, combine all of the ingredients in a small mixing bowl and reserve.

When you are ready to cook the scallops, heat a small sauté pan and add a bit of canola oil. Heat until almost smoking. Season the scallops with salt and curry powder. Sear each for about 2 minutes on each side without moving, until golden brown but opaque in the center. Remove the scallops from the pan and dab them on paper towels to remove excess oil. To plate, grab a nice flat white plate and, using the chive mayo in the squirt bottle, draw a circle around the plate's outer edge. Using the apple purée in the squeeze bottle, make four dime-sized dots on the inside of the chive mayo circle. Place 4 scallops on top of the apple purée, slightly off-center. Then divide the candied walnut salad into four portions and place a portion in the center of each plate. Garnish the plate with a few of your favorite herb leaves and serve.

TOMATO AND SPINACH ISRAELI COUSCOUS

2 tbsp (30 ml) extra virgin olive oil

2 tbsp (30 g) sliced garlic

½ onion, diced small

S&P Mix (page 133), to taste

2 cups (303 g) dried Israeli couscous

3 cups (720 ml) bone broth

1 preserved lemon, rind only, or 1 tbsp (6 g) lemon zest

3 tbsp (10 g) sundried tomatoes, chopped

1 tbsp (14 g) butter

1½ cups (368 g) fresh spinach, julienned

Okay, I realize the name of this recipe may not sound immediately exciting. But stay with me here. The whole time I was filming *Hell's Kitchen*, this was what I always chose to snack on. It's unbelievably tasty and goes with virtually anything as a side dish. Jamie Lauren—who was in the behind-the-scenes kitchen—came up with it, and we served it with Gordon's infamous lamb chops. (Don't make him ever ask, "Where is the lamb sauce!?")

Heat the olive oil in a small pot. Add the garlic and onion, sweat until soft, and season with S&P Mix to taste. Add the couscous and toast until lightly golden, about 2 minutes.

Add the broth, preserved lemon, and sundried tomatoes and bring to a boil. Reduce the heat to a simmer, add the butter, and season again with S&P Mix to taste. Place a lid on the pot and cook for 15 to 20 minutes. Once cooked, fold in the spinach and allow it to wilt before serving.

INFAMOUS HK LOBSTER RISOTTO

Pinch of salt

1 cup (197 g) arborio rice

2 tbsp (30 ml) extra virgin olive oil

8–10 cherry tomatoes

2 cloves garlic, minced

1 tbsp (10 g) minced shallot

¼ cup (60 ml) dry white wine

2 cups (480 ml) hot Rich and Flavorful Lobster Stock (page 166)

1 cup (145 g) lobster meat

2 tbsp (29 g) mascarpone

2 tbsp (12 g) lemon zest

1 tbsp (3 g) minced chives

1 tbsp (14 g) butter

S&P Mix (page 133), to taste

Parmesan wedge

2 tbsp (8 g) roughly chopped Italian parsley, for garnish

If you've ever watched *Hell's Kitchen*, then you know how iconic this risotto is. In fact, it's made the cut for 20 seasons! You probably also know how much the contestants screw it up. This isn't your normal way of making risotto, which is why it's so hard for the contestants to get right. But trust me when I tell you it's the best you'll ever have. I've adjusted the recipe to be very easy, versatile, and crazy-fast to make. You'll never make risotto any other way again. I know I haven't.

Blanch the arborio rice: Heat a pot of salted water as you would for cooking pasta. Once it has boiled, add the rice and give it a stir. Let it cook for 9 minutes. Remove from the heat and strain. Do *not* shock the rice, or rinse it in cold water, add any oil, or do anything to it! Just strain it and spread it out flat on a pan to cool.

In a large sauté pan, heat the olive oil over high heat until hot, then add the cherry tomatoes and cook just until blistered but not mushy, 2 to 3 minutes. Remove them from the pan and set aside. Reduce the heat to medium, add the garlic and shallot, and sweat until translucent, 2 to 3 minutes. Add the rice and stir for 30 seconds to evenly coat the rice with the mixture.

Deglaze with the white wine, which will also stop the garlic and shallots from overcooking. Add hot lobster stock incrementally in four portions, stirring constantly until the rice is just cooked. When the texture you like is achieved, add the lobster meat and heat just until it is warmed. Fold in the mascarpone, lemon zest, chives, and butter, and mix until well incorporated. Season with S&P Mix. Then, using a potato peeler, shave some Parmesan over the top. Add the blistered cherry tomatoes and garnish with chopped parsley.

MIXED FAMILY STYLE

The thing about eating, at least in my book, is that it always tastes better when you do it with people who are important to you. Yeah, I know, I know: That sounds so cheesy, I should serve it with crackers. But it's true. Some of the best food memories we have aren't great because the food was all that awesome, but because of who we ate it with. But what if—and bear with me now—it was both fantastic food *and* beloved company? Now you're in business! You'll find the keys to unlocking that magical combo in the pages that follow.

BRAISED PORK BELLY

2 tbsp (30 ml) canola oil

4 lb (1.8 kg) pork belly, skin on

S&P Mix (page 133)

2 Spanish onions, julienned

8 cloves garlic, smashed

4 sprigs rosemary

4 bay leaves

1 tsp chili flakes

½ tsp ground cloves

1 tbsp (15 ml) whole grain mustard

1 tbsp (8 g) yellow mustard seed

2–4 cups (480–960 ml) bone broth

Large-flaked sea salt, to taste, for serving

If you're on a diet, please turn the page. If you're on a pork diet, then look no further! This is the tastiest, meatiest, most unctuous piece of meat to ever hit your table, I assure you. The recipe yields a crispy-skinned top and soft, succulent meat. The braising liquid is a bit fatty (but amazing) and can be skimmed if you're using it immediately, or if you're saving some for later. Let it sit in your refrigerator for a bit and then remove the fat; you'll be left with the best sauce ever. I highly recommend serving the whole shebang with Crème Fraîche and Chive Potato Purée (page 158). Get in my belly, belly!

Preheat the oven to 325°F (163°C).

In a braising pan over high heat, add the canola oil. Score the pork belly skin with a knife and season liberally with S&P Mix, then sear the belly evenly on each side about 5 minutes. Remove the pork from the pan and sauté the onions and garlic until soft, about 5 minutes. Add the rosemary, bay leaves, chili flakes, cloves, whole grain mustard, and mustard seed, then place the pork on top, skin and fat side up. Add the broth until it's almost all the way up the pork belly, but not covering the fat on top. (This way the meat will braise and get soft, but the skin will roast and get crispy.) Cook for 3½ hours uncovered in the oven, or until the meat is very soft.

Remove it from the oven and let cool for 5 minutes in the liquid. Then remove the pork belly from the liquid and let rest for 5 more minutes.

Meanwhile, pour the braising liquid through a strainer and skim the fat off. Slice the pork belly with a serrated knife and sprinkle with some flaked sea salt. Serve immediately.

MAMA LE'S EGG ROLLS

MAKES ABOUT 3 DOZEN

8 oz (226 g) pork, ground

8 oz (226 g) shrimp, ground

½ cup (55 g) shredded carrot

1 cup (104 g) shredded taro

¼ cup (40 g) minced onion

¾ cup (105 g) thin cellophane rice noodles

2 tbsp (16 g) chicken bouillon powder

2 tbsp (25 g) sugar

1 tsp granulated garlic

1 tsp black pepper

1 tbsp (15 ml) sesame oil

1–1½ tbsp (15–23 ml) oyster sauce

1 egg, yolk and white separated into two bowls

3 dozen spring roll pastry or lumpia wrappers

My wife and her family are Vietnamese, and at the beginning of our relationship, her mom would make these for me (and my family) a lot because she considers them "entry level." Whatever level they are, they're incredible. I'm so obsessed with them, one Christmas her grandmother actually gave me a big bag of them, frozen—gift wrapped and everything! They're sized small, so they are perfect for a family dinner or for any cocktail party; just put them out on a platter and let people dip away. They're just a slam-dunk, all around. Thanks for the great recipe, Mama Le!

Make the filling: Mix the pork, shrimp, carrot, taro, onion, cellophane noodles, chicken bouillon powder, sugar, garlic, black pepper, sesame oil, oyster sauce, and the egg yolk in a large bowl.

Add 2 teaspoons (10 ml) of water to the bowl containing the egg white and beat with a fork until thoroughly mixed.

(continued)

1 qt (960 ml) canola oil, for frying

Salt

Hoisin sauce, Sriracha, or sweet chili sauce, for serving

Lay the pastry wrappers on a flat surface with the point facing up. Place about 1 to 1½ tablespoons (18 to 27 g) of filling right above the bottom point and roll 3 times. Then fold in the sides and roll as tightly as possible. Brush the egg white wash over the top point, so it seals and forms a cylinder. At this point you can freeze these and pull them out whenever you like. (I have bags of this stuff in my freezer ready to go at all times.)

If you've frozen the rolls, bring them out of the freezer a few hours before you're ready to fry, to defrost them. (Or just fry them freshly made.) To fry, heat the canola oil in a medium-sized pot to about 350°F (177°C), or you can also use a tabletop fryer. Place only a few rolls at a time in the oil, so as not to bring the temperature down too much. Fry them 10 to 12 minutes, or until golden brown and cooked throughout.

Once cooked, drain them on paper towels. I like to season them with salt as soon as they're out of the oil. (Note: This isn't traditional, and my mother-in-law might kill me.) Serve with hoisin sauce, Sriracha, or sweet chili sauce—or all of the above.

ITALIAN EGGPLANTIFICATION

EGGPLANT BREADING

2 large Italian eggplants

2–3 tsp (12–18 g) salt

Canola oil, for frying

4 cups (432 g) Italian breadcrumbs

1½ tbsp (12 g) garlic powder

1½ tbsp (8 g) grated Romano cheese

5 eggs

Let me start by saying that I've never liked eggplant Parmesan. It's always wet, greasy, flavorless, and covered with way too much cheese. But then my buddy Matt had me and my wife over for dinner one night, and he served us his version. *Boom!* My life changed forever! At the risk of sounding overly dramatic (too late!), this dish is something I literally think of and crave every day because it is light, it has tons of flavor, and you can actually taste the eggplant. It gave me a new lease on eggplant life. It isn't like any other I've ever had. What Matt served us was so effing good, I had no choice but to shake him down for the recipe. He's one of the best home cooks I know and is so very Italian, he's got paintings of pasta around his house. He probably should quit his day job and open a restaurant already. But in the meantime, at least I got his recipe.

Peel the eggplants and cut them into ⅛-inch (3-mm) rounds. Cover a dish with paper towels and lay the slices out in an even layer on top. Sprinkle about a teaspoon of the salt evenly over the top of the eggplant. Repeat the process, stacking layers of salted eggplant and paper towels on top of one another, and let it sit for about an hour. (Pro tip: Press gently with some extra cans of tomato to help drain even more liquid.) Don't rinse.

(continued)

TOMATO SAUCE

2 cloves garlic, minced

¼ cup (60 ml) extra virgin olive oil

2 (28-oz [794-g]) cans crushed tomatoes

1 tbsp (5 g) dried basil

2 tsp (12 g) salt

1 tsp chili flakes

1 tsp sugar

ASSEMBLY

8 oz (226 g) whole milk shredded mozzarella

½ cup (40 g) grated Romano cheese

¼ cup (15 g) fine-diced fresh parsley, for garnish

Meanwhile, make the tomato sauce: In a medium-sized, heavy-bottomed pot, sweat the garlic in the olive oil until translucent. Then add the crushed tomatoes, basil, salt, chili flakes, and sugar and simmer for 45 minutes. Keep the sauce warm until ready to use for the assembly.

After the eggplant is done draining, heat about ½ inch (1.3 cm) of the canola oil to about 325°F (163°C). In a bowl, mix the breadcrumbs with the garlic powder and Romano cheese. In a separate bowl, whisk the eggs.

Take the sliced eggplant, dip into the eggs and then the breadcrumbs, and gently fry on both sides until golden brown, 1 to 2 minutes per side. Drain and cool on a wire rack. (Note: You don't want to start with flour because it makes the breading too thick).

While the eggplant is frying, preheat the oven to 375°F (191°C).

To assemble, in a 9 x 13-inch (23 x 33-cm) pan, layer as follows: A layer of tomato sauce, then a layer of eggplant. Then a layer of mozzarella, then eggplant, more tomato sauce, and then Romano cheese. Repeat and finish with Romano (i.e., not the mozzarella) as the top layer.

Place the pan in the oven uncovered and cook for 25 to 30 minutes, or until it starts to bubble around the edges of pan. When finished, let it cool for at least 30 minutes. (Though, personally, I think it's best to let it sit overnight and reheat it gently the next day with any remaining sauce.) Garnish with a sprinkle of fresh parsley.

VEGETABLE LO MEIN

LO MEIN SAUCE
2 tbsp (30 ml) sesame oil

1 tbsp (6 g) minced ginger

1 tbsp (15 g) minced garlic

¼ cup (55 g) dark brown sugar

½ cup (120 ml) molasses

1 tbsp (15 ml) dry sherry wine

½ cup (120 ml) soy sauce

2 tbsp (30 ml) oyster sauce

2 tbsp (30 ml) rice wine vinegar

6 tbsp (90 ml) apple cider vinegar

1 tbsp (15 g) sambal

2 tbsp (16 g) cornstarch

3 tbsp (45 ml) cold water

VEGETABLE LO MEIN
2 tbsp (30 ml) canola oil

1 cup (70 g) sliced shiitake mushrooms

1 cup (160 g) sliced onion

1 cup (128 g) julienned carrot

1 cup (100 g) snow peas, cleaned

8 cups (2 kg) fresh lo mein noodles, blanched

¼ cup (12 g) chopped scallions, for garnish

2 tbsp (18 g) sesame seeds, toasted, for garnish

I know what you're thinking, "What's this white guy know about making Chinese lo mein?" Well I have yet to have better in any restaurant I have tried so far. So that is what I know! There's also no meat or seafood in this recipe, but feel free to add any of it if you want. To be honest, though, I don't even feel like I miss the protein in this dish at all. This is great warm, but I love it cold, too—as a chilled noodle salad. Bang! Two dishes in one. Magic!

Make the lo mein sauce: In a heavy-bottomed saucepan, heat the sesame oil over medium-high heat, and cook the ginger and garlic until they become fragrant, stirring frequently. Add the brown sugar, molasses, wine, soy sauce, oyster sauce, rice wine vinegar, apple cider vinegar, and sambal and bring to a boil. When the sauce is boiling, mix the cornstarch and water together in a separate bowl and quickly whisk into the sauce. This will thicken it and give it a nice velvety sheen. Reduce the heat to medium and let it simmer for 5 minutes. Remove from the heat. This will keep in your refrigerator for at least a month.

Make the vegetable lo mein: Heat the canola oil in a wok or large pan over medium-high heat. Add the mushrooms, onion, carrot, and snow peas. Stir fry until the vegetables are tender, 2 to 3 minutes. Add the lo mein noodles and lo mein sauce to taste. Cook for 3 minutes, until everything is well-coated in the sauce. Serve garnished with scallions and toasted sesame seeds.

BRAISED SHORT RIBS

with Banana-Mango Salsa

SERVES 4

1 tbsp (15 ml) canola oil

2 lb (907 g) boneless short ribs, cut into 4" (10-cm) cubes

S&P Mix (page 133)

1½ cups (360 ml) soy sauce

½ cup (110 g) light brown sugar

2 tbsp (30 ml) molasses

1 tbsp (15 ml) sesame oil

1 cup (240 ml) red wine

6 thin slices ginger

2 tbsp (30 g) minced garlic

1 cinnamon stick

2 star anise

½ cup (24 g) julienned green onions, divided, plus 2 tbsp (12 g) for garnish

2–3 cups (480–720 ml) bone broth

2½ cups (605 g) small-diced mango

½ cup (75 g) small-diced banana

1 jalapeño, seeds removed and minced

2 tbsp (30 ml) lime juice

2 tbsp (30 ml) maple syrup

2 tbsp (18 g) sesame seeds, toasted, for garnish

These days, short ribs are all the rage, all over the globe. You'll find them in an enormous variety of cultures all over the planet. My favorite way to serve them is with an Asian influence, and with a little bit of fruit to help cut the richness. The banana might sound a little weird but, I promise you, this recipe is so good you'll cry yourself to sleep after making it!

Heat the canola oil over high heat in a Dutch oven. Season the short ribs with S&P Mix and then sear them on both sides, until browned. Once seared, add the soy sauce, brown sugar, molasses, sesame oil, red wine, ginger, garlic, cinnamon stick, star anise, and ¼ cup (12 g) of green onions. Bring to a simmer over medium heat and season again with S&P Mix to taste. Add enough of the broth to cover the ribs and simmer, covered, for about 2½ hours or until fork tender.

Make the salsa: Combine the mango, banana, jalapeño, ¼ cup (12 g) of green onions, lime juice, and maple syrup together and season with S&P Mix.

Divide the salsa in half and spoon half onto four plates. Top each plate with the short ribs, and garnish with the remaining salsa. Spoon some of the braising liquid around the beef and garnish with the reserved green onions and toasted sesame seeds. Serve alone as an appetizer or with steamed rice as a main dish.

BACK PORCH GATHERINGS

We've all had those bittersweet days. When you finally get a day off, and miraculously, so do your friends. So, you decide—usually at the last minute—to try and pull off a barbecue. Or a deck party. Or a jam session around the fire pit. But then you realize it's actually a huge pain to get everything organized enough to make really good food at the last minute, so you just decide to punt and settle for making some mediocre burgers and bagged potato chips. And you wind up having fun even though the meal was pretty lame. Well, forget about ever doing that again. These backyard meals are fun to throw together and serve, and will be gobbled up faster than you can even mumble the word "leftovers."

REVERSE SEARED RIBEYE STEAK

with Wild Mushrooms, Compound Butter, and Fried Sage Salt

SERVES 3-4

TOMAHAWK STEAK

1 (36-oz [1-kg]) bone-in ribeye steak

1 tbsp (18 g) kosher salt

1 tbsp (7 g) paprika

1 tsp pepper

1 tsp garlic powder

1 tsp onion powder

1 tbsp (15 ml) canola oil

2 oz (57 g) butter

2 cloves garlic

2 sprigs thyme

One thousand percent, this fantastic dish simply had to be the cover recipe. This is the Cadillac, the Big Daddy, the Godzilla, the Fred Flintstone of all steaks. I mean honestly, what's better than a ginormous piece of perfectly cooked, well-seasoned, juicy steak that's topped with butter? Go ahead, think about it. I'll wait.

Pat the steak dry and place it on a wire rack over a rimmed baking sheet. Combine the salt, paprika, pepper, garlic powder, and onion powder in a bowl and apply the mix liberally to all surfaces of the steak. If possible, leave the steak uncovered and refrigerate overnight to "dry brine"—otherwise, leave the steak out with seasoning on it for 1 to 2 hours to come to room temperature.

When you're ready to cook the steak, preheat the oven to 225°F (107°C) and place the steak in the middle of the center oven rack. Cook until it reaches an internal temperature between 110 and 115°F (43 and 46°C) on a meat thermometer.

Heat a tablespoon (15 ml) of canola oil in a cast iron pan to medium-high heat on the stove. Transfer the steak to it, and cook the first side until browned and caramelized, then flip it and cook the second side. Add the butter, garlic, and thyme to the pan and use a spoon to baste the steak as it cooks.

Your steak is done when the internal temperature reaches 125°F (52°C) for rare, 135°F (57°C) for medium-rare, and 145°F (63°C) for medium. I will not allow you to cook it further than that, so please don't even think about it. Rest your steak for at least 15 to 20 minutes. When ready to serve, slice away from the bone and against the grain.

(continued)

WILD MUSHROOMS

2 lb (907 g) mixed wild mushrooms, irregularly chopped

½ cup (120 ml) extra virgin olive oil

2 shallots, diced small

4 tbsp (57 g) butter

S&P Mix (page 133), to taste

4 cloves garlic, minced

½ cup (30 g) chopped parsley

2 tsp (10 ml) soy sauce

2 tsp (10 ml) lemon juice

COMPOUND BUTTER

¼ lb (113 g) butter, softened

1 tbsp (15 ml) extra virgin olive oil

1 tbsp (15 ml) sherry vinegar

2 tsp (2 g) minced fresh chives

1 tsp minced thyme leaves

1 tsp minced sage leaves

1 tsp minced rosemary

FRIED SAGE SALT

4 tbsp (60 ml) canola oil, for frying

2 oz (57 g) sage leaves

2 tbsp (26 g) coarse sea salt

For the wild mushrooms, slice the small mushrooms on the thicker side and cut the large ones in a large dice. Heat the olive oil in a large pan or Dutch oven. Add the shallots and cook over low heat for 5 minutes, or until they're translucent. Add the butter and mushrooms, season with S&P Mix, and stir often over medium heat for 8 minutes, until they are tender and begin to release their juices. Stir in the garlic and cook for 2 more minutes. Toss in the parsley, soy sauce, and lemon juice and, if needed, season with S&P Mix again. Serve warm.

Make the compound butter: Mix all ingredients until well incorporated.

For the fried sage salt, in a small sauté pan, heat the canola oil and drop the sage leaves in. Fry until crispy. (Careful: The hot oil will spatter when the leaves are dropped in.) Reserve 6 to 8 leaves, then crush the rest and mix in with the salt.

To plate, fan slices out on the plate. Top with the compound butter and place the mushrooms on top and around the steak. Garnish with fried sage leaves and a healthy sprinkling of sea salt.

LACQUERED SALMON SIDE

with Celery and Green Apple Relish

1 (4-lb [1.8-kg]) skin-on side of filleted salmon

3 tbsp (42 g) brown sugar

3 tbsp (45 ml) molasses

3 tbsp plus 1 tsp (50 ml) Dijon mustard

3 tbsp (45 ml) balsamic vinegar

2 cups (220 g) green apple, julienned

½ cup (16 g) celery leaves

1 green onion, minced

1 tsp minced sage

½ cup (55 g) small-diced red bell pepper

¼ cup (60 ml) apple cider vinegar

I've never been a fan of salmon, to be honest, because it's so often overcooked and dry. But if cooked properly, I realized that it doesn't actually have to suck. Just the opposite: If you cook it right, it will take on a gorgeous silky texture and melt in your mouth. And although I don't usually order it out (for the reasons explained above), I do now make it at home for my family and friends—a lot. Don't be afraid of the whole side of salmon used in this recipe. It's cheaper than buying individual pieces, and once you've cooked it you can use the leftovers for salads, in salmon cakes, in pastas, and more. #mealprep2022

Preheat the oven to 350°F (177°C).

Remove the salmon from the refrigerator and let stand at room temperature for 10 minutes.

Make the lacquer: Combine the brown sugar, molasses, Dijon mustard, and balsamic vinegar and whisk until combined.

Make the celery and green apple relish: Mix the apple, celery leaves, onion, sage, bell pepper, and cider vinegar together. Set aside.

(continued)

¼ cup plus 1 tbsp (75 ml) extra virgin olive oil, divided

S&P Mix (page 133), to taste

5 sprigs rosemary

Line a large baking dish or rimmed baking sheet with a piece of aluminum foil. Lightly coat the foil with 1 tablespoon (15 ml) of the olive oil. Place the salmon on top. Drizzle the salmon with the remaining ¼ cup (60 ml) of olive oil and sprinkle with S&P Mix. Lay the rosemary on top of the salmon.

Bake the salmon for 15 to 20 minutes, until the salmon is rare-ish at the thickest part. (The cooking time will vary based on the thickness of your salmon. If your side is thinner—about 1 inch [2.5 cm] thick—then check several minutes early to ensure your salmon does not overcook. If your piece is 1½ inches [4 cm] or more, it may need longer.)

Remove the salmon from the oven. Change the oven setting to broil. Brush the lacquer over the fish to coat it thoroughly, then return the fish to the oven and broil for 3 to 5 minutes, until the top is nicely caramelized and the fish is cooked properly. Watch the salmon closely as it broils to make sure it doesn't burn. Remove it from the oven.

When you're ready to serve, season the relish with S&P Mix to taste. Spoon it on the side and top of the salmon and serve immediately.

JALAPEÑO RANCH BURGERS

CRISPY ONIONS

1 Spanish onion, peeled and thinly sliced into rings

1 cup (240 ml) buttermilk

1–1½ cups (125–188 g) all-purpose flour

2 tsp (4 g) Cajun Spice (page 137)

Canola oil, for frying

S&P Mix (page 133), to taste

BURGER

2 jalapeños, halved, seeds and stems removed

4 (8-oz [226-g]) 80/20 fresh, high quality beef patties

S&P Mix (page 133), to taste

8 slices Muenster cheese

4 brioche hamburger buns

¼ cup (57 g) butter, melted

8 heirloom tomato slices, sliced thick

1 cup (240 ml) Spicy Creole Ranch Dressing (page 141)

The Big Debate on how to cook burgers is whether to grill them or griddle them. I personally like mine griddled, and that's why my grill at home has been modified to be half-and-half. You can do it however you want. All I ask is that if you grill it, be careful not to over-char it, which makes it very dry and tough. The toppings on this burger are what elevate it, making it crunchy, creamy, spicy, and salty. It's the freakin' best! But you know what's not the best? Using frozen meat. So make sure you use fresh!

Make the crispy onions: Separate the onion slices with your fingers and place them in a bowl. Pour the buttermilk over them and let them sit for 10 minutes. In a separate bowl, mix the flour and Cajun Spice together.

Heat the oil to 375°F (191°C). Take a handful of the onions at a time, shake off the excess buttermilk, dredge them in the flour (making sure you shake off any excess) and add them to the hot oil. Fry them for a couple minutes, stirring them halfway through the cooking time to make sure every strand is crispy. Remove them from the oil and place them on a paper towel–lined plate. Season with S&P Mix. Repeat with the rest of the onions and set aside.

Make the burger: Preheat the grill to high. Place your jalapeños on the grill/griddle and cook until soft, then remove from the heat and mince them. Season the burger patties on both sides with S&P Mix, place on the grill/griddle, and cook to temperature, then melt the cheese on top. Brush the hamburger buns with melted butter, place on the grill/griddle, and toast evenly until golden brown. Place the toasted burger buns on a plate and begin to build your burger with the toppings (cheese, sliced heirloom tomato, Spicy Creole Ranch Dressing, minced jalapeños, and crispy onions) in order. Serve immediately.

GRILLED FLAMIN' HOT STREET CORN

1 (8½-oz [241-g]) bag CHEETOS® Crunchy FLAMIN' HOT® Cheese

1 cup (240 ml) mayonnaise

½ tsp liquid smoke

1½ tsp (7 ml) red wine vinegar

Pinch of smoked salt if you have it, or kosher is fine

6 ears corn

1 (½ cup [114 g]) stick butter, optional

1 tsp salt, optional

2 cups (480 ml) milk, optional

1 cup (120 g) cotija or queso fresco cheese, crumbled

4 small limes (Mexican or key limes are great, but any lime works), for garnish

6–10 sprigs cilantro, for garnish

This Mexican street corn is exciting, fun, delicious, and some may even say outrageous in the best possible way. It's a signature at my Mexican restaurant, Citrus & Salt and it has been the #1 seller now for almost four years. If it's not the best, coolest corn you've ever seen and tried, you can fight me!

Start by firing up your grill. (You could certainly roast the corn, but grilling gives it a much better flavor.)

Take your Flamin' Hot Cheetos and either crush them up fine in the bag—or you can just throw them in a food processor. You want it ground, but not to a powder. It should look like panko, not Italian breadcrumbs. Set the crushed Cheetos aside.

In a separate bowl, whisk the mayonnaise, liquid smoke, and red wine vinegar together. Season with the salt. Peel the corn and remove as much of the silky hairs as you can.

At this point you can either finish making the recipe and serve, or you can place the corn in the milk mix and hold for an hour or so until ready to serve. (I prefer it this way because the corn soaks up the milk and butter and that makes it taste amazing.) To do this, melt the butter in a small pot, then mix in the milk and salt before adding in your corn.

Cut the corn pieces in half and throw them on the grill as-is, until just lightly charred. Depending on your grill, this will take 5 to 10 minutes.

Once you're almost ready to eat, take the corn and roll it in the smoky mayo, then roll it in the Flamin' Hot Cheetos and place on a large plate.

Sprinkle the cheese over the top and garnish with lime (wedges if you're using big limes or halves if they're small limes) and cilantro sprigs. Serve immediately and make some friends!

CHARCUTERIE-TYPE THING

3 (4-oz [113-g]) balls whole burrata, drained if needed

½ tsp salt

Extra virgin olive oil or Buttermilk's Hot Honey (page 161)

Cracked black pepper, for garnish

1½ lb (680 g) assorted cured meats

4 (8-oz [226-g]) pieces of soft and firm cheeses

2 radish bunches, with greens on, trimmed and halved

8 oz (226 g) candied nuts

8 oz (226 g) dried fruit

8 oz (226 g) fig jam

8 oz (226 g) mixed olives

Toasted crusty bread, for serving

Grapes, for serving

Crackers, for serving

Dijon mustard, for serving

Charcuterie (not pronounced char-cuchi) isn't really a recipe, per se. Instead I like to think of preparing it as how a painter works with a canvas, and although everything is basically bought, it takes your imagination to make it look visually stunning with the proper presentation (see the photo for the stunning part). Every party needs one of these, and with the following guide, the sky's the limit, Picasso!

One of the most crucial steps in this recipe actually requires buying, not cooking. Buying the right combination of cured meats and types of cheeses will take it to the next level. I recommend finding at least three with different textures and flavors—a hard salami, for example, with a soft classic like mortadella, and then a prosciutto or country ham. Cheeses should also have varying textures and flavor profiles. A soft brie, say, works well with a salty, hard pecorino or a firm blue.

Make the whipped burrata: In the bowl of a food processor, combine the burrata and salt, and purée until smooth. Transfer to a serving bowl, drizzle with the olive oil or Buttermilk's Hot Honey, and garnish with cracked black pepper.

Assemble the charcuterie board: On a large cutting board or serving platter, arrange the whipped burrata with the cured meats, cheeses, radishes, nuts, dried fruit, jam, and olives around it. Serve with the bread, grapes, crackers, and mustard.

OVERSTUFFED BROWN BUTTER LOBSTER ROLLS

LOBSTER SALAD
3 lb (1.4 kg) fresh lobster meat (claw and knuckle meat works best)

¼ cup (40 g) minced shallots

¼ cup (25 g) minced celery

¼ cup (12 g) minced chives

1½–2 cups (360–480 ml) Brown Butter Mayonnaise (page 149)

S&P Mix (page 133), to taste

ASSEMBLY
8 tbsp (114 g) butter, softened

8 brioche split-top hot dog buns

Old Bay seasoning, for dusting

Promise me something, okay? When you're buying lobster, make sure it's fresh and not frozen. Most places that serve lobster rolls use frozen because it's cheaper (and don't get me wrong, they can still be really good). But, but, *but*: Once you use fresh, you can—and will—never go back. Look, I know lobster is expensive. But if you're going to make this, then pass on the frozen; you'll just do your efforts in the kitchen a disservice. And hey, if I'm wrong, you can send a sternly worded email to my publicist (and I'll kindly ask her to forget to reply). No, but seriously: In this case, there's just no substitute for fresh.

Make the lobster salad: Mix the lobster meat with the shallots, celery, and chives. Fold in the Brown Butter Mayonnaise and season with S&P Mix to taste. Keep in the refrigerator until ready to use.

Toast the buns: Spread the softened butter on each side of each bun, dust with Old Bay seasoning, and place in a pan or griddle over medium heat. Toast until golden brown and warm throughout.

Once the buns are toasted, divide the lobster salad equally among the buns and serve immediately.

RISE

– AND –

SHINE

In my experience, there are breakfast people and anti-breakfast people. There are brunch people, too, and they tend to sit somewhere in between the first two. But enough gastronomic stereotyping; let's talk about the food itself. At the beginning of the day, I'm a big fan of leaning into either salty—as in, leek and prosciutto strata (page 99)—or sweet— see gingerbread pancakes (page 93) and Strawberry-Basil Ricotta Toast (page 94). It's all delicious enough to make a breakfast person out of an anti-breakfast one. Or a brunch person out of a breakfast one. . . . Oh, never mind: Just cook and eat some of the following recipes, and I guarantee you won't care what time of day it is.

GINGERBREAD PANCAKES

with Strawberry-Maple Salsa and Sweet Mascarpone

SERVES 4

STRAWBERRY-MAPLE SALSA

8 large strawberries, washed, hulled, and diced

½ cup (120 ml) maple syrup

Pinch of ground cinnamon

GINGERBREAD PANCAKES

2 cups (250 g) all-purpose flour

2 tbsp (28 g) dark brown sugar

1½ tsp (7 g) baking powder

½ tsp baking soda

1 tsp kosher salt

2 tsp (4 g) ground ginger

2 tsp (6 g) ground cinnamon

¼ tsp nutmeg

¼ tsp ground cloves

1 cup (240 ml) milk

¼ cup (60 ml) brewed coffee

2 eggs

3 tbsp (42 g) butter, melted

1 tbsp (15 ml) lemon juice

TOPPINGS

6 tbsp (87 g) sweet variation of mascarpone (see page 153)

6 sprigs mint

Powdered sugar

I was going to ask for a story from the gingerbread man about this, but word is you can't catch him.

Make the strawberry-maple salsa: Mix all of the ingredients together in a bowl and set aside.

Make the pancakes: In a large bowl, whisk together the flour, brown sugar, baking powder, baking soda, salt, ginger, cinnamon, nutmeg, and ground cloves. In a separate bowl, whisk the milk, coffee, eggs, melted butter, and lemon juice until well combined. Add the wet ingredients to the dry ingredients and gently stir until combined. Having some lumps is good. You don't want to overmix this; if it's too incorporated it won't be as fluffy.

Heat a lightly greased griddle or nonstick skillet over medium-low heat. Ladle about 4 ounces (113 g) of the batter at a time into the pan, and cook until it starts to bubble on the surface and the edges start to brown, 1 to 2 minutes. Then carefully flip. Cook on the other side until the batter is completely cooked through. Continue until all the batter is used.

Top with your favorite sweet variation of mascarpone, strawberry-maple salsa, and mint sprigs, and dust with powdered sugar.

STRAWBERRY-BASIL RICOTTA TOAST

WHIPPED RICOTTA

1 cup (246 g) very high-quality ricotta

½ cup (116 g) mascarpone or, for a sweet option, replace with Brown Sugar Mascarpone (page 153)

Pinch of salt

STRAWBERRY JAM

1 lb (454 g) strawberries, hulled

¼ cup (50 g) sugar

1 strip of lemon peel

1 cup (240 ml) water

ASSEMBLY

2" (5-cm)-thick slices of bread (I like sourdough, challah, or brioche)

6–8 tiny basil leaves

In all honesty, I am not a giant "toast" guy. But this one right here is legit. I've got a few adjectives to describe what I think of it: sweet, savory, smooth, creamy, simple, elegant, delicious, addictive, easy, silky, lovely, wonderful, scrumptious, delectable, luscious, and . . . okay, I'll stop.

To make the whipped ricotta, place all of the ingredients in a food processor and whip until the mixture is smooth and fluffy.

To make the strawberry jam, cut the strawberries in half and macerate in sugar for about 15 minutes. Place into a pot with the lemon peel and water and cook on low to medium heat, stirring occasionally to prevent burning, for about 20 minutes. This will make about 2 cups (480 ml).

To assemble: Toast the bread slices and cover with a generous portion of ricotta, topping with the strawberry jam and basil leaves. Serve immediately.

DANISH ALMOND-PEAR COFFEE CAKE

Butter, for greasing the pan
1 cup (125 g) all-purpose flour, divided
1 cup (96 g) almond flour
¼ tsp salt
1 tsp baking powder
1 cup (200 g) sugar
2 eggs
½ cup (114 g) butter, melted
⅔ cup (160 ml) milk
2 tsp (10 ml) vanilla extract
2 tsp (10 ml) almond extract
2 pears, peeled, cored, and sliced

This is no run-of-the-mill, nothing-to-write-home-about coffee cake. It comes from my co-author, Alexandra Hall, whose Danish family eats it for breakfast, as a dessert after lunch and dinner, and as a snack anytime in between. (So basically, they just eat it all day.) The butter-and-vanilla-heavy cake is delicious enough itself, but it's the almond and cinnamon topping—gooey in some parts, crunchy and almost candied in others—that puts it way over the top. Don't be surprised if you start eating it long past brunchtime, too.

Preheat the oven to 350°F (177°C). Grease a 9-inch (23-cm) springform pan with butter, and dust the inside with 2 tablespoons (16 g) of the all-purpose flour, rotating it while tapping to cover the entire inside. Shake out any extra flour.

In a large bowl, stir the remaining all-purpose flour, almond flour, salt, and baking powder.

In another large bowl, mix the sugar and eggs with a mixer on medium speed for 3 to 4 minutes, until you've got a light, pale mixture. Add the melted butter and the milk—both in a slow, steady pour—while still mixing. Add the vanilla and almond extracts. Mix to completely combine, and then slowly add the flour mixture until combined.

Spread the pear slices on the bottom of the prepared cake pan. Pour the batter over them to cover, and use a spatula to spread the batter evenly.

(continued)

TOPPING

6 tbsp (85 g) butter, cut into chunks
¾ cup (81 g) sliced almonds
½ cup (100 g) sugar
¼ tsp kosher salt
2 tbsp (16 g) all-purpose flour
2 tbsp (30 ml) milk
½ tsp ground cinnamon
½ tsp ground cardamom

Place the pan on top of a baking sheet (so the topping doesn't spill over into your oven when it bakes later) and bake for 40 minutes.

Ten minutes before the 40 minutes is up, make the topping: In a medium saucepan, heat all of the topping ingredients over medium heat. Stir constantly for 7 to 10 minutes—it will start bubbling a bit—until it thickens enough to coat the back of a spoon.

Quickly remove the cake from the oven, and carefully pour the topping all over it. Put the cake back in the oven to bake until the topping is a beautiful golden brown, another 15 to 20 minutes.

Transfer the baking sheet to a cooling rack, and let sit for 5 to 6 minutes. Before the topping has hardened completely, carefully run a knife or a spatula between the cake and the pan sides to separate them, then open up the springform pan to release the cake.

Let the topping harden before cutting the cake into individual pieces to serve.

LEEK, PROSCIUTTO, AND SWEET POTATO STRATA

SERVES 6

1 tbsp (14 g) butter, plus more for greasing the baking dish

3 lb (1.4 kg) sweet potato, peeled and diced into ½" (1.3-cm) pieces

2 tbsp (30 ml) extra virgin olive oil, divided

2 tbsp (4 g) finely chopped thyme

1 tsp S&P Mix (page 133), plus more to taste

Strata is (or should be, at least) one of the great secret weapons of any kitchen. It's easy to make, and also uses up all kinds of leftovers and orchestrates them into a delicious symphony. Once you've got the base ingredients in place—bread, eggs, and half-and-half—you can add whatever you have sitting around in your fridge. It's best to go for a combination of one type of meat (bacon, ham, or sausage are especially great), one green veggie (spinach, artichoke, and the like), one or two kinds of cheese, and maybe another veggie like onion, mushrooms, potato, or pepper. In this version, the sweet potato adds a richness, the leeks bring a fresh and oniony flavor, and the prosciutto adds . . . well, hey, it's prosciutto. So basically, anything it touches is going to taste incredible.

Preheat the oven to 350°F (177°C). Use the butter to grease a 9 x 13-inch (23 x 33-cm) baking dish. In a large bowl, toss the sweet potato with 1 tablespoon (15 ml) of the olive oil and the thyme. Season with S&P Mix to taste. Spread the sweet potato on the baking sheet in a single layer and roast for about 25 minutes, until tender, tossing once halfway through. Set aside and let cool.

(continued)

3 leeks, white and light green parts, thinly sliced

10 eggs

2½ cups (600 ml) half-and-half

¼ cup (25 g) freshly grated Parmesan cheese

8 oz (226 g) baguette, cut into ½" (1.3-cm) dice

4 oz (113 g) prosciutto, thinly sliced

While that's baking, in a medium skillet, melt the butter with the remaining tablespoon (15 ml) of olive oil. Add the leeks and season with S&P Mix to taste. Cook over medium heat, stirring until just tender, 15 to 20 minutes.

In a large bowl, beat the eggs with the half-and-half, and add the cheese and 1 teaspoon of S&P Mix. Stir in the bread and let soak for 10 minutes. Fold in the sweet potato, leeks, and the prosciutto. Pour the mixture into the baking dish and bake for roughly an hour, until golden on top. Slice into equal segments and serve immediately.

OVERNIGHT SPICED CHALLAH FRENCH TOAST

SERVES 4-6

½ cup (120 ml) heavy cream

5 large eggs

2 cups (480 ml) whole milk

2 tsp (10 ml) vanilla extract

2 tsp (10 g) sugar

½ tsp lemon zest

½ tsp ground cinnamon

½ tsp ground cardamom

Pinch of salt

1 loaf challah or brioche, cut into 1" (2.5-cm) slices

6 tbsp (85 g) butter, divided

It's unbelievable, the kind of magic that happens overnight in this decadent dish. Soaking the sweet and soft challah (or brioche) in the liquid custard gives it a deliciously smooth and creamy texture in the center, with crusty, buttery edges that crunch after being crisped up in the oven. You'll never look at French toast the same way again.

The night before you're going to serve this dish, make the custard: In a large bowl, whisk together the cream, eggs, milk, vanilla, sugar, lemon zest, cinnamon, cardamom, and salt.

Arrange the challah slices in an even layer on a rimmed baking sheet. Pour the custard on top, and let it sit at room temperature for an hour. Carefully turn the bread over, and let sit in the refrigerator overnight.

When ready to serve, in a large nonstick pan over medium heat, melt 2 tablespoons (28 g) of butter. Add several pieces of the bread to the pan and cook 4 to 5 minutes until golden brown on the bottom.

Turn each over and cook again until golden brown. Repeat with the remaining 4 tablespoons (57 g) of butter and bread. Serve hot, and top with your favorite fruits, syrups, or jams—and maybe some chocolate chips and whipped cream for good measure.

DESSERTIVORE

At the end of a fantastic meal, is there anything more blissful than a simple and bright-flavored final course? I love a dessert that spotlights the true flavors of fruit and custard, or fruit and chocolate, or fruit and pastry. . . . You get it, right? I dig fruit. It makes the dish sing with all kinds of sharp and sweet, tart and citrusy, or rich and beguiling flavor. My bet is you'll get addicted to some (if not all) of these recipes. I mean seriously, if my Nana's Apple Pie (page 108) doesn't hook you for life, I'll eat my hat. Or, actually, I'll just eat another piece of her pie. . . .

PISTACHIO-RASPBERRY PARFAIT

RASPBERRY PURÉE
1 lb (454 g) raspberries
6 tbsp (75 g) sugar
¼ cup (60 ml) water

WHIPPED CREAM
1¼ cups (300 ml) heavy cream
2 tbsp (16 g) powdered sugar

ASSEMBLY
12–14 (1½" [4-cm]) meringue cookies, crumbled, divided
6 oz (170 g) raspberries
6 tbsp (38 g) finely chopped toasted pistachios
Edible flowers or mint sprigs, for garnish

Fresh, simple desserts like this one are my jam (literally, in some cases). This one has a cool, smooth texture, boasts big flavor, and is visually stunning. Meanwhile, it's unbelievably easy to whip up—you can either make them individually or as a large format for a gathering. Feel free to get creative with the fruit choice; it's fun to mix it up. Maybe I'll try a fig and hazelnut version next!

For a richer parfait, incorporate Brown Sugar Mascarpone (see page 153) into the layers.

Make the raspberry purée: Add all the ingredients to a small pot and cook over medium heat until it's reduced about halfway and has a syrupy consistency. Strain out the seeds and allow it to cool.

Make the whipped cream: Pour the heavy cream in a small bowl and whip until soft peaks form. Add the powdered sugar gradually and beat until stiff peaks form. Set aside.

In a separate bowl, place ¾ of the crumbled pieces of meringue and gently fold the whipped cream into the meringue. Now fold in the raspberry purée to give a streaky effect. Don't overmix—you want it to have colorful swirls. Separate evenly into four clear bowls and layer with whole raspberries and pistachios. Top with edible flowers or mint sprigs as well as the remaining meringue pieces.

NANA'S APPLE PIE

with Buttermilk Whipped Cream and Caramel Crème Anglaise

CRUST

2½ cups plus 2 tbsp (328 g) all-purpose flour
½ cup (120 ml) canola oil
5 tbsp plus 2 tbsp (105 ml) cold milk, divided

FILLING

8 Cortland apples, peeled, cored, and medium diced
½ cup (100 g) sugar
1¼ tsp (4 g) cinnamon
¼ tsp nutmeg
2 tbsp (28 g) butter, melted

As little kid, for as far back as I can remember, I used to watch my Nana make this during the holidays. It's one of my favorite memories. Thankfully, she passed the recipe down to my mom, so we get to keep on eating her amazing and delicious pie. The recipe is so incredibly simple and has minimal ingredients, but it's just perfect. I have, however, added the buttermilk whipped cream and caramel crème anglaise to make it a bit more cheffy, and to take it from perfect to perfect-er. Miss you, Nana!

Preheat the oven to 375°F (191°C).

Make the crust: In a large bowl, gently mix the flour, canola oil, and 5 tablespoons (75 ml) of milk with a fork until the dough forms. Wrap the dough in plastic wrap and chill while you make the filling.

Make the filling: Mix all of the ingredients together in a large bowl.

Roll out the crust: Divide the chilled dough in half and place each half between two pieces of wax paper about 10 inches (25 cm) long. With a rolling pin, roll across the top piece of wax paper until the dough is large enough to cover a 9-inch (23-cm) pie tin. Mold the bottom crust into the pie tin, then add the filling on top and spread evenly around the bottom crust. Place the second crust on top, covering the filling, and crimp the edges around the pie (with either a pie crimper or by pinching it with your fingers). Break off any excess dough and reserve it in case patching is necessary. Cut six slits in the middle of the top of the pie. Brush the crust with the remaining 2 tablespoons (30 ml) of milk.

Bake for 45 to 50 minutes, then cool on a baking rack.

(continued)

BUTTERMILK WHIPPED CREAM

2 cups (480 ml) heavy whipping cream

¾ cup (180 ml) buttermilk

1 tbsp (8 g) powdered sugar

1 tsp pure vanilla extract

CARAMEL CRÈME ANGLAISE

2 cups (480 ml) half-and-half

1 vanilla pod, scraped or 1 tsp vanilla extract

5 egg yolks

½ cup (100 g) sugar

¼ cup (60 ml) caramel sauce

Make the whipped cream: Beat all the ingredients until stiff peaks form, and keep in the refrigerator until ready to serve.

Make the crème anglaise: In a medium saucepan over medium heat, bring the half-and-half and vanilla to a simmer. Whisk the yolks and sugar together in a medium bowl, until the mixture becomes light and pale in color. Slowly whisk in the hot half-and-half mix, and then return the mixture to the pot. Cook over medium heat, stirring constantly with a wooden spoon, until the mixture coats the back of the spoon. Stir in the caramel sauce, then strain it into a bowl and set over an ice bath. Stir until chilled. Cover and refrigerate until cool.

To serve, place a healthy slice of pie (chilled or warm) on your plate, then drizzle with the crème anglaise and top with a dollop of buttermilk whipped cream.

BLUEBERRY BISCUIT BREAD PUDDING

with Whiskey Sauce

BREAD PUDDING

5 eggs

1 cup (220 g) brown sugar

8 cups (1.9 L) milk

1 cup (240 ml) heavy cream

¼ tsp cinnamon

½ tsp vanilla extract

Butter, for greasing the pan

5 buttermilk biscuits, torn into pieces

2 cups (296 g) blueberries

Okay, ready? Three things about the following recipe: 1) This bread pudding is so good, you may not ever make another. 2) Any booze will basically work for it in place of the whiskey, so feel free to swap it. 3) Biscuits make everything better, and that's completely true of this dessert. (If you want to make your own, see—and feel free to buy—my previous cookbook, *Buttermilk & Bourbon: New Orleans Recipes with a Modern Flair*, for an incredible buttermilk biscuit recipe.)

Make the bread pudding: In a large bowl, make a custard mixture by whisking the eggs until well blended. Add the brown sugar and mix it in, then add the milk, heavy cream, cinnamon, and vanilla extract. Use the butter to grease an 8 x 8-inch (20 x 20-cm) square baking dish and lay the torn biscuits in it. Sprinkle the blueberries around, and then pour the custard mixture over the biscuits and blueberries. Cover the dish with foil and let it soak for 45 minutes in the refrigerator.

Preheat the oven to 325°F (163°C). Poke holes in the foil and bake until the bread pudding is set up, about 40 minutes. Then remove the foil and bake another 10 minutes to brown the top lightly.

(continued)

WHISKEY SAUCE

2 tbsp (28 g) butter

1 tsp cinnamon

1½ cups (330 g) dark brown sugar

5 tbsp (75 ml) whiskey

½ cup (120 ml) heavy cream

WHIPPED CREAM

1¼ cups (300 ml) heavy cream

2 tbsp (16 g) powdered sugar, plus more for dusting

While it's baking, make the whiskey sauce: In a small saucepan, melt the butter and whisk in the cinnamon, brown sugar, and whiskey. Continue whisking until the mixture boils, then add in the cream. Whisk quickly to incorporate, then remove and let cool. Pour the sauce into a squeeze bottle.

Make the whipped cream: Pour the heavy cream in a small bowl and whip until soft peaks form. Add the powdered sugar gradually and beat until stiff peaks form. Cover and refrigerate until ready to serve.

To serve, squeeze several dollops of the whiskey sauce on a dessert plate. Scoop out the desired portion size of the pudding, placing it on the sauced plate. Dust the pudding with powdered sugar and finish it with a dollop of the whipped cream.

SIMPLE FANCY
CITRUS PUDDING

2 Meyer lemons (if you can't find Meyer lemons at your local store, substitute with the zest and juice of 1 lemon and 1 orange, mixed together)

1 envelope unflavored gelatin

¼ cup (60 ml) cold water

1¼ cup (250 g) sugar, divided

1 cup (240 ml) boiling water

3 eggs, whites and yolks separated, divided

Pinch of salt

½ quart (480 ml) milk

1 tbsp (8 g) cornstarch

1 cup (24 g) fresh basil leaves, divided

Grated dark chocolate, for garnish

I think the name says it all. Ice cold pudding in a bowl is comfort in a glass, and a touch of citrus makes it pop. Use this on its own or as a component to another dish. You can always do what my wife does and eat a bite of cake with a spoonful of pudding at the same time. Makes sense.

Make the pudding: Zest the lemons and set aside the zest. Juice the lemons. In a small bowl, dissolve the gelatin in the cold water. Add the Meyer lemon juice, 1 cup (200 g) of the sugar, and boiling water. Let it sit until it's syrupy, about 45 minutes.

In a seperate bowl, beat the egg whites until they form soft peaks, then keep beating as you pour in the gelatin until the whole mixture is fluffy, 5 to 6 minutes. Chill a large bowl by running cold water over and in it in the sink, and then spoon the egg white mixture into it. Cover and chill in the refrigerator for at least 4 hours.

While the pudding sets, make the basil custard sauce: Fill a large bowl with ice water and set aside. In a saucepan, whisk the egg yolks, the remaining ¼ cup (50 g) of sugar, and salt. Once that's blended, stir in the milk, cornstarch, and ¾ cup (18 g) of the basil leaves. Cook over low heat, stirring constantly and slowly, until it's thick enough to coat the back of a spoon and a thermometer reads 160°F (71°C), for 6 to 7 minutes. Quickly pour through a strainer into a bowl. Place the bowl into the larger bowl containing the ice water for about 5 minutes, letting the water come about two-thirds of the way up the sides of the custard bowl. Cover the custard and refrigerate for at least 30 minutes.

When ready to serve, scoop out the desired portion of pudding into a bowl. Pour the custard sauce over the top, and garnish with a pinch of the Meyer lemon zest, 1 or 2 of the remaining basil leaves and the dark chocolate.

WHITE CHOCOLATE LEMON COOKIE CUSTARD

8 oz (226 g) white chocolate chips

½ cup (120 ml) egg yolks

1¼ oz (35 g) sugar

1 cup (240 ml) milk

1 cup (240 ml) heavy cream

6 small lemon cookies of your choice, crushed, for garnish

1½ tsp (3 g) lemon zest, for garnish

¼ cup (31 g) toasted macadamia nuts, crushed, for garnish

I know most people will disagree with me, but I've always loved white chocolate more than regular chocolate. That's fine; you've got a right to your opinions. But this is my cookbook, and I'm making this recipe a white chocolate–based one. So, you can either write your own damn cookbook, or just go ahead and make this recipe but substitute your chocolate of choice for the white (and hurt my feelings).

Make the custard: Pour the white chocolate chips into a medium-sized, heat-safe bowl and set aside. In a separate bowl, whisk the egg yolks until they're well mixed. Add the sugar in gradually, whisking until the mixture is a pale yellow and slightly thick. Meanwhile, in a large pot, bring the milk and heavy cream to a boil. Pour that directly over the white chocolate chips and whisk to incorporate.

Temper the hot chocolate mixture, constantly stirring it while you gradually add in the egg yolk mixture.

Once it's completely mixed together, return it to the pot and cook to 180°F (82°C), whisking continuously.

Immediately pour the mixture into six small bowls and chill until ready to serve.

When the custard is firm, garnish each bowl with crushed lemon cookies, lemon zest, and macadamia nuts.

EYE-OPENERS

In running my restaurants, I've been beyond lucky enough to work with some of the world's most talented bar managers and bartenders. (I see you, Sarah Baker and Samantha Gray!) They've been inspiring to work with in conjuring up the coolest ways to create and serve concoctions that our diners flock to—from chocolatey twists on an old-fashioned (page 122) to an outrageously refreshing sangria (page 121). The coolest part is these are easy to make and will make you look like you have been a mixologist for years. Bottoms up!

WATERMELON-ROSÉ SANGRIA

3–4 large watermelon pieces, cubed

¼ oz (7 ml) fresh squeezed lemon juice

¼ oz (7 ml) fresh squeezed lime juice

½ oz (15 ml) agave syrup

½ oz (15 ml) St. Germaine liquor

5 oz (148 ml) of sparkling rosé

1 orchid or edible flower, for garnish

Powdered sugar, for garnish

1 watermelon wedge, for garnish

I love a good summer cocktail. Hell, I love any cocktail in pretty much any season, for that matter. This one is all about the technique; you can always change the fruit, or change the rosé to a Cava, Prosecco, or even Champagne, if you fancy. And it can be adapted for any time of year because there's always a great seasonal fruit to use, and the sparkling wine just lifts it to a new and refreshing level. Long story short, it's versatile and terrific for any occasion. (Unless you're allergic to fruit, then you're screwed.)

In a cocktail shaker, add the watermelon cubes, lemon juice, lime juice, agave syrup, and St. Germaine. Shake vigorously. Strain into a 16-ounce (473-ml) wine glass full of ice. Top with sparkling rosé. Garnish with the orchid dusted with powdered sugar, the wedge of watermelon, and a really fun straw.

CHOCOLATE PRALINE OLD-FASHIONED

1 cup (220 g) packed brown sugar

1 cup (240 ml) water

½ cup (50 g) toasted pecans

1 tbsp (15 ml) honey

1 tbsp (5 g) unsweetened cocoa powder

2 oz (57 ml) bourbon of your choice

4 dashes (2 ml) chocolate bitters

2 dashes (1 ml) angostura bitters

1 Luxardo Original Maraschino Cherry, for garnish

Sarah Baker is one of the most creative bartenders I've ever had the pleasure of working with. She oversees two of my restaurants' beverage programs and is an absolute Jedi behind the bar. She's been working on perfecting this drink for a long time. Yes, it does have some cocoa in it, but don't let that put you off; it's about creating a balance, and using that balance to let the bourbon shine.

Make the pecan praline simple syrup: In a small saucepan, simmer the brown sugar, water, and toasted pecans on low for 10 minutes. Strain and cool.

Dip the rim of a highball glass in honey and then into unsweetened cocoa powder, and add ice to the glass.

In a separate shaker filled with ice, add the bourbon, 1 ounce (30 ml) of the pecan praline simple syrup, and both bitters. Stir for 30 seconds. Strain into the prepared highball glass. Garnish with a Luxardo cherry.

If you'll have some leftover simple syrup, save it for a future drink. It will keep in an airtight container in the refrigerator for about a month.

THE ELIXIR

¼ cup (60 ml) honey

¼ cup (60 ml) hot water

½ teaspoon cayenne pepper, to taste

1½ oz (44 ml) bourbon of choice

½ oz (15 ml) fresh lemon juice

1 (12-oz [355-ml]) can ginger beer

1 sprig rosemary, for garnish

This drink's a staple at my Boston restaurant, Buttermilk & Bourbon. One sip and you'll know why: It's mysterious and a totally tasty alchemy. The honey's sweetness and the kick of the bourbon and cayenne get amped up even further by the ginger beer's spice. And the smoky rosemary garnish not only adds big flavor and an alluring scent, but it also makes for a drinking sensation you won't soon forget.

Dissolve the honey in the hot water and add the cayenne, adjusting to how spicy you prefer it.

In a shaker, add the bourbon, cayenne honey mixture, lemon juice and shake. Fill a glass with ice and pour it all in. Top with ginger beer to almost the top.

Garnish with the sprig of rosemary, and lightly burn the herb's top needles with a lighter until it smokes.

3 A.M. ON
FRENCHMAN STREET

MAKES 1 COCKTAIL

¼ cup (60 ml) maple syrup

½ cup (60 g) walnut halves

Pinch of salt

2 tbsp (30 ml) pure maple syrup, divided

1½ oz (44 ml) whiskey (Uncle Nearest 1884 Small Batch is my favorite for this)

¾ oz (22 ml) coffee liqueur

2 dashes (1 ml) black walnut bitters

Samantha Gray has been by my side for four-plus years now as the bar manager at the Buttermilk & Bourbon location in Boston. She's been responsible for our unbelievable cocktails from creation to execution. I trust her 100 percent—she's a giant asset to my restaurant. And this is her favorite cocktail. Sure, it's a touch more work than a gin and tonic, but who wants to be basic, anyway?

Make the maple-glazed walnut rim: Heat the maple syrup in a skillet over medium-high heat. Toss in the walnuts and salt. Stirring often, let it cook for about 3 minutes until the syrup is caramelized and the nuts are toasted. Remove from pan and let it cool on a non-stick surface. Once the walnuts are cooled, muddle them into a crumble.

On a plate, pour out 1 tablespoon (15 ml) of maple syrup and dip the rim of a glass into it and then into the walnut crumble. Let sit.

Make the drink: Combine the whiskey, coffee liqueur, 1 tablespoon (15 ml) of maple syrup, and black walnut bitters in a separate mixing glass. Add ice and use a stirring spoon to mix the ingredients until the glass is chilled. Strain into the rimmed rocks glass to serve.

KING CAKE SHOT

CINNAMON SIMPLE SYRUP
1 cup (200 g) sugar
1 cup (240 ml) water
3–4 cinnamon sticks

1 oz (28 ml) vodka
½ oz (15 ml) cinnamon simple syrup
½ oz (15 ml) cream soda
Whipped cream, for garnish
Pinch of yellow sugar, for garnish
Pinch of green sugar, for garnish
Pinch of purple sugar, for garnish

When is the last time you saw a recipe for a shot in a cookbook? Never, you say? Correct! We are cutting edge here at *Simple Fancy* headquarters. My three favorite things about this are: 1) Super fun. 2) Looks awesome. 3) Tastes fantastic. The colored sugar makes it resemble a Louisiana king cake, but it honestly tastes just as good without it. Especially if you are drinking alone. I won't tell anyone . . . loser.

Make the cinnamon simple syrup: Bring all the ingredients to a boil, then let cool and remove cinnamon sticks. You should have 1½ cups (360 ml).

Combine the vodka, cinnamon simple syrup, and cream soda in a shaker. Pour into a shot glass. Garnish with whipped cream and decorative sugar.

– MY –

PANTRY STAPLES

Consider the following recipes for outrageously good brines, rubs, dips, and dressings to be the true rock stars in your repertoire, the greatest weapons in your culinary arsenal. Without them, even the most carefully braised lamb shank or perfectly al dente pasta would taste, well, just blah. Learn to make and reach for these, and your dishes will always boast that extra something, that *je ne sais quoi* that makes them memorable standouts.

S&P MIX

2 cups (576 g) kosher salt

½ cup (67 g) coarse grind black pepper (18 mesh grind)

What I'm about to share with you is very controversial: 90% of chefs out there do *not* premix their salt and pepper together. But I do. I am brave!

That's because one of my first jobs was working for James Beard Award–winning Chef Chris Schlesinger, and that's how he did it. It's what he taught me, and I've never looked back. You obviously don't need to do the same, but I think it's much more convenient to have the right proportions already on hand as you're cooking. So wherever you find the "S&P Mix" throughout this book, it refers to this recipe.

Mix both ingredients together. Store in an easily accessible canister that, when you need to, you can open with one hand while you're cooking with the other.

CHARRED ONION AND BLUE CHEESE RELISH

MAKES ABOUT 1 CUP (250 G)

4 cloves garlic, smashed

2 tbsp (30 ml) balsamic vinegar

4 tbsp (60 ml) extra virgin olive oil, divided

1 sprig rosemary, chopped

1 tbsp (15 ml) whole grain mustard

S&P Mix (page 133), to taste

1 medium red onion, cut into ½" (1-cm) rings

2 tbsp (17 g) blue cheese, crumbled

Make this once, and you'll use it forever. Serve it as a warm relish, or add a bit more olive oil and use it as a vinaigrette. Or serve it warm over a nice steak. It's that versatile and couldn't be easier to make. Basically, keep it handy in your arsenal for whenever you want to impress.

Combine the garlic, vinegar, 2 tablespoons (30 ml) of the olive oil, rosemary, and mustard in a mixing bowl and season with S&P Mix. Pour over the onions and marinate for a minimum of 1 hour but no more than 24.

Heat a grill. Remove the onions from the marinade, reserving the remaining liquid. On the hot grill, grill the onions until they're lightly charred, 6 to 8 minutes. Strain the reserved liquid. Place the onions in a food processor and pulse, then mix back into the strained liquid and add the remaining 2 tablespoons (30 ml) of olive oil. Season again with S&P Mix.

You can either leave out the blue cheese and warm the onion mixture slightly before folding in the cheese just before serving, or fold in the blue cheese and serve it chilled.

CAJUN SPICE

½ cup (56 g) paprika
½ cup (36 g) dried basil
½ cup (22 g) dried thyme
½ tsp cayenne pepper
¼ cup (48 g) gumbo filé powder
2 tbsp (36 g) kosher salt
2 tbsp (16 g) chili powder
1 tsp ground bay leaves

Everyone has their own version of Creole/Cajun/blackening rub, and this is mine. Actually I have a few, but this is the simplest and most flavorful one that I think you should have in your arsenal. This will easily last a couple of months if you keep it airtight, but if the spices in it become stale at any point, just toast it all in a pan for a minute and that will bring it right back to life.

P.S. Don't skip on the gumbo filé powder; it can be hard to find, but it's worth seeking out. But if you don't feel like making the effort, feel free to half-ass it and just buy some salty, flavorless Cajun spice at the store instead. See if I care. It will still work—just don't hold me responsible.

Mix everything together well and seal in an airtight container.

BLACK PEPPER BACON BITS

1 cup (112 g) bacon bits
1½ tsp (3 g) ground black pepper, divided

Bacon is the thing that dreams are made of. I love the added black pepper in this; the smoky, spicy quality is everything and is great on a salad or soup. There is a reason you hear people say, "Bacon makes everything better." I put it on ice cream last night and it's still true.

Preheat the oven to 300°F (149°C). Mix the bacon with 1 teaspoon of black pepper and spread on a cookie sheet. Bake for 20 minutes or until crisp. Strain the fat and toss in the additional ½ teaspoon of black pepper. Store at room temperature in a sealed container.

SPICY CREOLE RANCH DRESSING

1 cup (240 ml) mayonnaise

2 tbsp (30 ml) Crystal hot sauce

1 tbsp (4 g) Cajun Spice (page 137)

½ cup (120 ml) buttermilk

1 tbsp (15 ml) red wine vinegar

1 tbsp (4 g) minced fresh parsley

1 tbsp (3 g) minced fresh chives

1 tbsp (4 g) minced fresh dill

1 tbsp (7 g) onion powder

1 tsp celery salt

S&P Mix (page 133), to taste

You love ranch dressing, I love ranch dressing, we all love ranch dressing! This recipe is so good and very easy to adjust, as well. Remove the Cajun Spice and you have a basic buttermilk ranch. Or add avocado and you have an avocado ranch. Add roasted tomato and you have . . . you get where I'm going with this.

Whisk all the ingredients in a bowl and season with S&P Mix. The dressing will keep for at least a week in the refrigerator.

CHIPOTLE HOLLANDAISE SAUCE

½ lb (226 g) unsalted butter

2 cloves garlic, minced

4 egg yolks

½ lemon, juiced

1 tbsp (16 g) chipotle purée or paste

2 tsp (10 ml) Worcestershire sauce

2 tsp (4 g) Cajun Spice (page 137)

Salt, to taste

Hollandaise is the man . . . or woman! They don't call this a mother sauce for nothing. You learn how to make it on day one in culinary school for a reason; once you've mastered it, there are so many variations and so many ways to use it. And yeah, I know what you're thinking: It's hard to make. It's a lot of butter. It's complicated. Well, you know what? Lock it up! It's easy, it's fun to make, you can easily change the flavors, and if you're worried about all the butter, you can always just use it sparingly.

Add the butter and minced garlic to a small saucepan and melt slowly to infuse the butter and cook the garlic.

In a food processor or blender, combine the egg yolks, lemon juice, chipotle purée, and the Worcestershire sauce. While the machine is running, slowly drizzle in the warm butter mixture and slow in a steady stream until emulsified and creamy. Add the Cajun Spice and season with salt. Serve immediately or gently keep warm until needed.

RED REMOULADE

1 cup (240 ml) mayonnaise

½ cup (120 ml) ketchup

3 tbsp (18 g) finely minced celery

2 cloves garlic, minced

1 tbsp (15 g) horseradish

1 tbsp (4 g) minced parsley

3 tbsp (45 ml) whole grain mustard

¾ cup (180 ml) red wine vinegar

¾ cup (180 ml) rice wine vinegar

¾ cup (84 g) paprika

½ cup (120 ml) Crystal hot sauce

S&P Mix (page 133), to taste

This is *the* sauce of the south. I love it because it's so spicy, so creamy, so vinegary, and so very vibrant all in one. It's terrific as a dipping sauce, or on anything, anywhere in place of mayonnaise. (I also love it on my fries—just FYI in case you wanted to make some for me.)

Whisk all of the ingredients together in a medium bowl, and season with S&P Mix to taste.

PASTRAMI BRINE

1 gallon (3.8 L) hot water

4 ribs celery, diced

2 oz (57 g) ground coriander

1½ tbsp (11 g) ground white pepper

1½ tbsp (15 g) granulated garlic

½ cup (146 g) kosher salt

½ cup (110 g) brown sugar

1 oz (28 g) pink curing salt

1 cinnamon stick

½ cup (48 g) pickling spice

Protein of choice, such as beef, pork, or fish

You're probably wondering why I'm including a recipe for a pastrami brine when there's no other recipe to use it with in this cookbook. But I love (and use) this brine so much, I figured you needed it in your life. I use it on all kinds of meats—not just beef—to incorporate pastrami's flavor profiles into as many dishes as I can, and I recommend you do the same. (And for the record, I like mayo, not mustard, on my pastrami sandwich.)

In a large pot, mix all the ingredients together with the hot water and chill before adding whichever protein you'll be brining. Brine beef for a minimum of 48 hours, chicken and pork 24 hours, and fish 3 to 4 hours. Then remove.

BROWN BUTTER MAYONNAISE

1 stick butter (½ cup [114 g])

1½ (360 ml) cups mayonnaise

2 tbsp (30 ml) lemon juice

1 tbsp (4 g) minced fresh herbs (parsley, chives, tarragon, or chervil will work)

S&P Mix (page 133), to taste

Anyone who knows me knows that mayonnaise is one of my favorite things on earth. But then mix some butter in with it and OMG you've got a masterpiece on your hands. This is unbelievably fantastic as a topping or a dipping sauce for any seafood and can just as simply be used instead of mayo for a sandwich.

In a small pot over medium heat, melt the butter. Once melted, reduce the heat to medium-low and continue cooking, watching closely and stirring occasionally. It will simmer and start to turn brown. Once the simmering stops and the butter is brown and smells nutty, remove from the heat and let cool slightly.

Whisk the cooled brown butter and mayonnaise together in a bowl, then add the lemon juice, add the herbs, and season with S&P Mix to taste.

HOT CHICKEN
SPICE RUB

1 cup (82 g) cayenne pepper
¼ cup (73 g) salt
⅓ cup (32 g) dry mustard powder
3 tbsp (38 g) sugar
3 tbsp (21 g) smoked paprika
3 tbsp (20 g) ground black pepper
2 tbsp (20 g) granulated garlic

I call this Hot Chicken Spice Rub for two reasons: yes, because it's hot, but also because it's straight-up magical when you're making Nashville hot chicken. But in all honesty, it's my go-to seasoning anytime I want to make something sit-up-and-take-notice spicy. It's well balanced, definitely isn't messing around on the flavor front, adds nice color to any dish, and all in all, is just a key thing to have kicking around when you need some heat in your life!

Mix all ingredients and store in a container in a dry place. It will keep for up to 1 month.

VARIATIONS OF MASCARPONE

You're not going to find someone else out there like me, who has zero Italian in them but loves mascarpone as much I do. I could and would (and have) eaten it with a spoon right out of the container. It's like cream cheese and butter had a beautiful, angelic baby. It's so versatile that it can be eaten sweet or savory and used on anything from a bagel to a dessert or even as a garnish on pasta. You'll see it a lot in this book—just like you'd see it a lot in my fridge. Here are five different variations, both sweet and savory.

Whisk all the ingredients in a mixing bowl until light, fluffy, and well combined. Store it in a sealed, tight container in the refrigerator and it will last about a week.

SWEET VARIATIONS

BROWN SUGAR
1 pint (464 g) mascarpone

2 tbsp (28 g) light brown sugar

½ tsp vanilla bean paste or extract

DULCE DE LECHE
1 pint (464 g) mascarpone

¼ cup (60 ml) dulce de leche or caramel if you can't find it

Pinch of salt

NUTELLA
1 pint (464 g) mascarpone

½ cup (120 ml) Nutella

½ tsp vanilla bean paste or extract

SAVORY VARIATIONS

BASIL-BLACK TRUFFLE
1 pint (464 g) mascarpone

2 tbsp (6 g) minced fresh basil

½ cup (96 g) canned black truffle peelings, chopped

1 tsp salt

1 tbsp (15 ml) white truffle oil

LEMON-CHIVE
1 pint (464 g) mascarpone

1 tbsp (3 g) fresh chopped chives

1 lemon, zested and juiced

½ tsp lemon pepper

ALSO LEARN

Much like my pantry staples in the previous chapter, the recipes that follow are the building blocks for countless incredible dishes. You may use these a little less often (the lobster stock, page 166, for example, or the Pickled Red Onions, page 162) than the staples, but they're still an extremely worthy move to keep in your back pocket.

CALABRIAN CHILI CHIMICHURRI

1 cup (240 ml) canola oil
½ cup (120 ml) Calabrian chili oil
¼ cup (60 ml) red wine vinegar
¼ cup (60 ml) lemon juice
8 cloves garlic, minced
2 bunches parsley, leaves picked and chopped
3 tbsp (30 g) minced red onion
1 bunch cilantro, leaves picked and chopped
2 tbsp (11 g) oregano, dried
2 tbsp (30 g) chopped Calabrian peppers
S&P Mix (page 133), to taste

It's fresh, it's vibrant, and it is phenomenal on any cooked meat. All right, I lied: It's actually phenomenal on almost anything—meat fish, chicken, vegetables, etc. I thought this was something you should also learn just to have it in your back pocket.

Combine all ingredients except the S&P Mix and stir with a fork until well incorporated. Season with S&P Mix to taste.

CRÈME FRAÎCHE AND CHIVE POTATO PURÉE

2 lb (907 g) Idaho potatoes, peeled and quartered

½ cup (120 ml) heavy cream, warm

¼ lb (113 g) butter, diced and kept cold

½ cup (120 ml) crème fraîche

¼ cup (12 g) chopped fresh chives

Salt and white pepper, to taste

The name of this dish may sound super bougie, but in reality we're just making some amazing mashed potatoes. My father-in-law is from Vietnam and is not a huge fan of "American" food, but he always asks me to make this at the holidays. Feel free to change the flavoring as well—maybe add in some Cheddar and bacon, or Parmesan and garlic. Let your imagination go wild.

Place the potatoes in a large pot with enough water to cover. Bring to a boil, and cook for 20 to 25 minutes until fork tender. Drain, and then run through a ricer for a super smooth purée (or mash with a potato masher for a more rustic look). Mix in the warm cream and cold butter. Don't overmix. Stir in the crème fraîche and chives, and season with salt and white pepper to taste.

BUTTERMILK'S HOT HONEY

1½ cups (360 ml) honey
¼ cup (60 ml) Crystal hot sauce
1 tbsp (9 g) Hot Chicken Spice Rub (page 150)

We use this a lot at my restaurant, Buttermilk & Bourbon. I'm always thankful to have it around, since it adds a nicely balanced sweetness with just a touch of heat. Drizzle it on biscuits, chicken, cheese, shrimp, vegetables, and just about anything else you want.

Put all of the ingredients in a medium saucepan, and bring the mixture to a simmer. Remove from the heat, and store it at room temperature—it will keep for months.

PICKLED RED ONIONS

1 lb (454 g) red onions, sliced very thin

2 cups (480 ml) red wine vinegar

1 cup (240 ml) water

2 tsp (12 g) salt

1 cup (200 g) sugar

Tangy, crisp, and the kind of topping that can take a dish from *Zzzzzzz* to wide awake. Pickled red onions make all the difference on burgers, in salads and sandwiches, in tacos, and nestled up next to fried fish and steaks.

Place the onions in a large bowl.

In a large saucepan, bring the vinegar, water, salt, and sugar to a boil together. Lower the heat to bring the mixture to a gentle simmer over medium heat, then carefully pour the liquid over the onions. Let sit for a minimum of 2 hours (ideally overnight). Kept covered and refrigerated, the onions will keep for 2 to 3 weeks.

SOUR CREAM CAESAR DRESSING

MAKES ABOUT 3 CUPS (720 ML)

1 cup (240 ml) mayonnaise

1 clove garlic, minced

2 anchovies, minced

1 tbsp (15 ml) lemon juice

1 tbsp (15 ml) Worcestershire sauce

1 tbsp (15 ml) red wine vinegar

1 tbsp (15 ml) Dijon mustard

4 tbsp (20 g) Romano cheese

4 tbsp (60 ml) sour cream

2 tbsp (30 ml) water

S&P Mix (page 133), to taste

It is said that Caesar Cardini created the iconic salad in 1924 in Mexico. But rumor has it that Jason Santos made the dressing better in 2019. Make this and love it more than any other dressing you have ever had. If you disagree, please send correspondence to salad@ceasardressing.com.

Mix everything together except the S&P Mix, and then season with S&P Mix to taste.

RICH AND FLAVORFUL LOBSTER STOCK

1 tbsp (15 ml) canola oil

1 onion, peeled and cut in large chunks

2 ribs celery, cut in large chunks

2 carrots, peeled and cut in large chunks

3 cloves garlic

2 tsp (8 g) black peppercorns

1 star anise pod

4 sprigs thyme

4 bay leaves

½ tsp chili flakes

2 tbsp (32 g) tomato paste

Shells from 2–3 lobsters

1 cup (240 ml) dry white wine

1 gallon (3.8 L) water

Truth be told, I think lobster stock may be my favorite stock of all. It's huge on lobster flavor and tastes expensive. It's my go-to whenever I want to really add some serious richness to a seafood dish.

In a large pot or pan, heat the oil and lightly sauté the onion, celery, carrots, and garlic, until the onion starts to turn translucent, about 5 minutes. Add in the peppercorns, star anise pod, thyme, bay leaves, chili flakes, and tomato paste, and cook for 1 to 2 minutes.

Add the lobster shells, mix everything with a large spoon, and cook until the lobster shells turn bright red, 5 to 8 minutes. Deglaze the pot with the white wine, then add enough of the water to cover.

Bring the pot to a boil, then turn it down to let it simmer for 1 hour. Strain the stock through an all-purpose fine-mesh strainer. Cool the stock and refrigerate for up to 4 days, or freeze immediately once cooled.

CRISPY SOFT-BOILED EGGS

6 eggs
½ cup (63 g) flour
1 beaten egg
½ cup (28 g) panko breadcrumbs, puréed fine
Canola oil, for frying

Eggs are so versatile, and we have all cooked an egg or two in our day, but I never see soft-boiled anywhere. It's like an over easy egg but cooked in the shell, white cooked but yolk runny. These are my favorite, and I am starting a campaign to bring back the soft-boiled egg.

In a boiling pot of water, carefully place the eggs with a large spoon and cook precisely for 7 minutes. Remove them with a slotted spoon and place in a bowl of ice water to immediately stop the cooking.

Peel each egg and roll in the flour, then in the beaten egg, then in the panko crumbs.

In a pot, heat 1½ inches (4 cm) of canola oil to about 350°F (177°C). Fry the eggs until crispy and just golden brown—be careful not to overcook, so that the yolk stays runny. Serve warm.

ACKNOWLEDGMENTS

A heartfelt thank you to the following people:

Once again, to my wife. Thuy: Thank you for being the best thing to ever happen to me. You're always my biggest supporter. You inspire me to push every day to get better and better. I love you so much. And most of all, thank you for always letting me pursue my dreams.

To my mom: You've been my #1 fan since day one. You've always encouraged me to do what I love, and you've always been there, being just the best mother a son could ask for. Your selflessness is second to none, and I love you.

To my in-laws, Helen and Brandon Le: You guys are the greatest and make it so easy to be a part of the family.

To Jill, Steve, John, and Maureen: Thank you for being so supportive and always being there when I need you.

To Jack and Billy: More years, more restaurants. I wouldn't be here if it weren't for you two.

To my publicist, Nicole: Thank you for putting up with me and always pushing me out of my comfort zone. You've always believed in me, and I can't thank you enough.

To my co-author and friend, Alex: Thank you for being so organized and for the patience you've had with me. I couldn't/wouldn't have done this book in a million years without you. The next ten are going to be great. ☺

To Jeff: I have so much to say, but I think you already know what you do for me and the business. I 100% wouldn't be able to do this without you. (Hey, wanna do another one?!)

To Erica: Thank you for dealing with me and all my crazy ideas. We would not be operating at this level if it weren't for you.

To Kelly, Liz, and Henry: You guys are the ones that deserve all the praise. Your hard work, dedication, and willingness to do what it takes is outstanding! My hat's off to you.

To Doug (aka Enrique): Thanks for always saying yes to anything I ask of you. You are the best, and we wouldn't have these amazing restaurants without you.

To Ken Goodman, a gentleman and a scholar: You're incredible at what you do. Thank you for caring so much and making the first photo just as important as the last.

To Lish Steiling: Thank you for making my simple food look so fancy and for being the coolest, most down-to-earth chef I have ever met.

To all my amazing staff: Thank you for all your hard work and dedication. Thank you for believing in our brand and, most importantly, choosing to believe in me.

To Page Street Publishing: You're the best! You've made my dream come true . . . twice!

One of Boston's most creative and charismatic chefs, the blue-haired Jason Santos has wowed guests with his innovative cuisine and larger-than-life personality at his four bustling restaurants. They include Nash Bar, Buttermilk & Bourbon Boston, Buttermilk & Bourbon Watertown, and Citrus & Salt.

While other kids grew up watching *Sesame Street*, Chef Jason Santos grew up experimenting in his grandmother's kitchen watching (and idolizing) Julia Child. It was during his early years in the kitchen that Santos realized his passion for cooking, which he will spend the rest of his life cultivating.

Following his success cooking in many of Boston's best restaurants, Santos competed on Season 7 of Fox TV's hit television show, *Hell's Kitchen*. Santos's charisma and culinary expertise quickly secured him as a fan favorite and garnered the attention of one of the industry's top critics, Chef Gordon Ramsay. His successful run on the show concluded with a runner-up finish and a newfound national recognition. Jason will be returning to *Hell's Kitchen* as Chef Ramsay's sous-chef for the Blue Team for his fourth season.

Santos now divides his time as owner and executive chef at Nash Bar, a sleek, two-floor southern restaurant and country music venue that is in the heart of Boston's Theater District; Buttermilk & Bourbon (Boston and Watertown), New Orleans–influenced restaurants with as much character and charm as the city itself; and Citrus & Salt, a coastal Mexican restaurant in Boston's Back Bay.

Santos is also a recurring guest on the *Today Show*, *Live with Kelly and Ryan*, CBS TV's *The Talk*, *CBS This Morning*, and subsequent seasons of *Hell's Kitchen*. Santos also appears regularly on the popular Paramount TV hit show, *Bar Rescue*, where he rehabilitates failing restaurants and bars as the chef-expert alongside Jon Taffer.

In March of 2019, Santos debuted his first cookbook, *Buttermilk & Bourbon: New Orleans Recipes with a Modern Flair*, which is available at bookstores across the nation and on Amazon. Santos lives in Woburn, Massachusetts, with his wife, Thuy, and splits his time between running his restaurants, writing cookbooks, performing media appearances, attending culinary events, and dreaming up his next signature dishes.